The Christian Vision
of Humanity

Basic Christian Anthropology

John R. Sachs, S.J.

A Michael Glazier Book
THE LITURGICAL PRESS
Collegeville, Minnesota

Acknowledgments

This book was begun one summer at Fairfield Univerity. A sabbatical from the Weston School of Theology, the Jesuit Theology Center where I teach, and the generous support of the Louis Bannan, S.J., Foundation for Christian Values at Santa Clara University enabled me to finish it. I would like to express my heartfelt gratitude to the Jesuits at these institutions and to the Bannan Foundation for their encouragement and support.

A Michael Glazier Book published by The Liturgical Press

Cover Art: Master Bertram (1350–1415): The Grabow Altarpiece. Detail: The Rest on the Flight into Egypt. Kunsthalle, Hamburg.

Library of Congress Cataloging-in-Publication Data

Sachs, John Randall.
The Christian vision of humanity / by John R. Sachs.
p. cm. — (Zacchaeus studies. Theology)
"A Michael Glazier book."
Includes bibliographical references.
ISBN 0-8146-5756-7
1. Man (Christian theology) I. Title. II. Series.
BT701.2.S242 1991
233—dc20
91-12957
CIP

Contents

Editor's Note

This series of short texts in doctrinal subjects is designed to offer introductory volumes accessible to any educated reader. Dealing with the central topics of Christian faith, the authors have set out to explain the theological interpretation of these topics in a Catholic context without assuming a professional theological training on the part of the reader.

We who have worked on the series hope that these books will serve well in college theology classes where they can be used either as a series or as individual introductory presentations leading to a deeper exploration of a particular topic. We also hope that these books will be widely used and useful in adult study circles, continuing education and RENEW programs, and will be picked up by casual browsers in bookstores. We want to serve the needs of any who are trying to understand more thoroughly the meaning of the Catholic faith and its relevance to the changing circumstances of our times.

Each author has endeavored to present the biblical foundation, the traditional development, the official church position and the contemporary theological discussion of the doctrine or topic in hand. Controversial questions are discussed within the context of the established teaching and the accepted theological interpretation.

We undertook the series in response to increasing interest among educated Catholics in issues arising in the contemporary church, doctrines that raise new questions in a contemporary setting, and teachings that now call for wider and deeper appreciation. To such people we offer these volumes, hoping that reading them may be a satisfying and heartening experience.

Monika K. Hellwig
Series Editor

Introduction

The year 1990 marked the twenty-fifth anniversary of the promulgation of *Gaudium et Spes*, the *Pastoral Constitution on the Church in the Modern World*. In a way quite astonishing for its time, and still prophetic for Christians of today, the Second Vatican Council situated its reflection on the faith of the church directly in relationship with the joys and hopes, the real griefs and anxieties of the world, especially of those who are poor or afflicted in any way. The message of the Gospel and the call to faith do not refer to some eternal, spiritual realm unconnected with the men and women of earth and their problems. On the contrary, Christianity believes and proclaims the salvation of *this* world in Christ. In order to be able to preach the Gospel effectively, the church recognized its responsibility to understand the world and to address its real problems, hopes and longings.

Human hopes and anxieties in every age have raised questions about our origins, possibilities and the ultimate meaning of life. We do not ask such questions idly; our experience forces us to ask them. We often try to avoid them, for as adults, we become aware of the paradoxes and contradictions in life, the fragility of all answers and the great possibility that there are no final answers.

Our recent history is a record both of incredible artistic, scientific and technological achievement and of unimaginable cruelty, evil and human suffering. But, as Pope John Paul II's encyclical *Sollicitudo Rei Socialis* (1988) reminds us, the great advances which continue to change our world and ourselves at an ever-increasing rate have not necessarily made our world more human. The "progress" of human civilization has brought about the power to exploit earth's resources and peoples. The very existence of our planet is threatened by the nuclear weapons we use to ensure "peace." World-wide problems of poverty and starvation grow larger. We cannot blind ourselves to the real evil which continues to mark our world.

On other levels, often more keenly felt because they hit people personally and directly, we experience the vulnerability and contradictions of life in natural catastrophes, plane crashes, AIDS, the failure of marriages, the abuse of children, cowardice, addiction and the debilitation of sickness and old age. Looking deep within or at the world outside, aware of the immense suffering, brokenness and disillusionment in human lives, all of us wonder whether or not our hopes and dreams, our labors and accomplishments, are really leading somewhere.

Our experience of life is profoundly paradoxical. At times we can find much in ourselves or in others which makes it easy to stand high and feel that we are indeed "little less than the gods," as Psalm 8 puts it. At other times we find much that cuts us down at the knees and makes it difficult to believe in anything. And at the end, death stands waiting to cut us down. Nonetheless, the long history of human hope, love, labor and struggle continues. It is testimony to our conviction that our lives do make sense, that we and our world are truly becoming something, that there is a real future.

We sense that this process of becoming moves toward its future, not simply according to "natural processes" or some predetermined plan. We realize that we are capable of and responsible for shaping it.

But just what is this future? What is really possible? What can we truly hope for, both for ourselves personally and for the world as a whole? Upon what or whom can we ultimately rely, especially where we must face our own limits and failures? Here is where the question about what it means to be human leads in some form or other to the question about God and salvation.

The Biblical Vision

Of course, our questions do not of themselves produce faith in anything. Biblical faith expresses the conviction that God has graciously revealed God's self in our history as the Lord, Creator and Savior of the world. The "answer" of the Scriptures to the questions about the ultimate nature and meaning of human life is a long story which begins with the experience of Semitic slaves who are led out of slavery in Egypt into freedom as a people with a new land and future. It is beautifully recounted in the liturgical form of an ancient creed in Dt 26:5-11. It was this event, culminating in the Covenant on Sinai, which forged them into a people and revealed to them who the God of their ancestors was. It also revealed to them who they were for God. They were a people of the Promise; a people of the Covenant. Throughout the OT, we find Israel's reflection, remarkable for its frank honesty, on God's loving faithfulness despite its own infidelity and subsequent enslavement. The prophets called Israel to repentance; the Promise and Covenant were renewed in the promise of one who would come to establish a kingdom of unending peace, justice and freedom. Whether through a kingly messiah or a suffering servant, the focus is on the fact that God is at work. God's reign will bring final justice and peace. The Kingdom of God brings together the whole OT story about God's Promise and the world's life.

The NT understands itself as the culmination of this story precisely as the confession of Jesus as the one who was to come. In his life, death and resurrection, Christian faith perceives the personal presence and action of God. In a variety of ways, the different Gospels present Jesus as the transforming fulfillment of the OT Promise and Covenant, even though he does not quite fit the categories of Israel's expectations. Contrary to the implication of Jesus' rebuke to the disciples on the road to Emmaus, the idea of a suffering messiah is foreign to the OT. It was just as hard for Jesus' listeners to accept the real "paradigm shift" in the parables Jesus used about the Kingdom. He spoke about God's justice and love in a manner that seemed blasphemous to some, utterly ridiculous to others. The way he spoke about and associated with people, especially the poor, the marginalized and the sinners was just as shocking. Even more than the prophets before him, he preached the boundlessness of God's love and the universal scope of God's Covenant.

Jesus understood himself and his entire life in terms of a unique, final and unsurpassable mission to announce and establish God's

Kingdom. For Christian faith, the Kingdom which Jesus preaches is the fulfillment of God's Covenant Promise and the consummation of God's plan for creation. It is the final realm of life and salvation into which all men and women are invited to enter. Only God's justice, only God's love has the power to conquer the powers of sin and death and to bring human beings to the wholeness and fullness of their humanity.

The establishment of God's justice, which would at last bring healing and wholeness to a broken world, had been a central theme of the prophets before Jesus. But Jesus stands out uniquely when compared with them precisely in the way he connected his mission, the Kingdom, with his own person. This is seen in his unparalleled, even blasphemous claim to authority, even with respect to the Torah (Matthew 5). But perhaps most dramatic is the way Jesus linked his hearers' response to him and their final fate before the Son of Man who would come to judge (Mk 8:38).

Christian faith proclaims that Jesus and God are one. In Jesus himself, the Kingdom has appeared. The gracious mercy and love which constitute God's justice is victoriously established. In Christ, we see that God's reign is the loving union between God and humanity. Christ is both the "image of the unseen God" (Col 1:15) and the "final Adam" (1 Cor 15:45), the one in whom we can see our final end. From before all time it was God's plan to form us to his image (Rom 8:29). In Christ, God "tells" us that human flesh and blood is capable of divine life. Our real humanity, the same humanity which Jesus shared, is destined for a share in God's own divine nature (2 Pet 1:4).

The Human and the Human World according to Vatican II

Christian faith, therefore, has a particular vision of the world and of humanity, a vision that is founded upon the relationship between God and God's creation as revealed in the person and ministry of Jesus Christ. *Gaudium et Spes,* which I have already mentioned, sets forth a basic Christian anthropology in its first three chapters. The key elements are found in (1) the inviolable dignity of every human person, (2) the essential centrality of community and (3) the significance of human action.

The *dignity* of all men and women, created in God's image, is grounded in their unique relationship of intimacy with God (12). Human persons are spiritual, embodied creatures (14-15) who, above all, are blessed with freedom which, guided by conscience (16), comes to its fulfillment in love of God and neighbor. Because this freedom has been damaged by sin and is threatened by death, it can only come to its fulfillment through God's grace (13, 17). Its fulfillment is an endless sharing in God's own divine life (18). Because the dignity of human persons is rooted and perfected in God, faith's recognition of God is not hostile to human freedom and dignity, as some forms of atheism claim. Christians must work with all who labor for the dignity of human beings and basic human rights (19-21). In a spirit of dialogue and cooperation, they look to Jesus Christ, the final Adam, where for the eyes of faith, the mystery of humanity is revealed (22).

The dignity of every human person does not diminish the fact that one can be human only in *community* with others. Apart from relationships to others, we can neither live nor develop. From the very beginning humanity is created as community and all men and women are called as a single family to universal communion with one another and with God (23-24). This requires a social order based not on individualist ethic (30) but on the common good. It must be "founded on truth, built on justice, and animated by love" (26). Social structures must grow from and express a basic reverence for others, especially for those who think or act differently, so that the basic equality of all is recognized (27-29), and the fruitful participation of all in society is ensured (31).

Human action is understood to be an unfolding of God's own creative work (34). Therefore, Christian faith demands that human beings labor to build up the world, attending to the genuine good of the human race and so develop themselves as truly human persons according to the divine plan (35). The rightful autonomy of the different arts and sciences is willed by God and to be respected by all (36). Christians will, however, adopt a critical attitude in their endeavors recognizing the real and pervasive power of sin. The perfection and happiness which God wills for the creation cannot be identified naively with "progress," especially where technology is developed and implemented without moral principles (37). Finally, the transformation of the world can come only from the power of love. Convinced in faith that the effort to bring about a universal communion of justice and peace is not a hopeless one, the church summons believers to dedicate themselves to the service of the earth and its peoples and so to prepare for that final act in which God will receive the world and bring it to perfection as God's Kingdom (38). The expectation of the "new earth" is precisely what should strengthen concern for cultivating this earth, in which the Kingdom is already present and growing in mystery (39).

These are the main themes of a Christian anthropology. In the following chapters I will reflect on them in greater detail. We know much about ourselves from other disciplines which investigate the human being from particular points of view (physiological, genetic, psychological, political, economic and so on). And yet, rapidly increasing specialization makes the need for a comprehensive view of human persons, our role in the universe, fundamental human values and our ultimate destiny more crucial than ever. This is what a theological anthropology attempts to do, considering human persons precisely in terms of their relationship to God. Taking seriously what all these other perspectives have to tell us, it can illumine and challenge them. For Christian faith recognizes that the God-given dignity of the human person, realized in community with others, in loving care of God's world, is the very heart of the gospel.

1

Creation in God's Image

I have tried to present at least the basic contours of a Christian vision of humanity in the context of our ordinary experience of the paradoxes and contradictions of life. Christian faith is a recognition that God's Word, Jesus Christ, speaks to our ultimate questions about meaning and life, particularly as we are threatened by the realities of evil, suffering and death. To those who believe in him, Jesus reveals who God truly is, who we truly are and what we and our world are finally to become.

Now it is time to look more closely at the basic elements of this vision. In this chapter I would like to turn to one of the central themes of the stories found in the first chapters of Genesis: creation.

Of course, creation is not a notion unique to the Bible. It arises from the universal human experience of contingency and the question such experience raises about our origins. Ordinary experience teaches us that we do not bring ourselves into existence and that we do not have the power to keep ourselves in existence. All around we see beginnings and ends. We wonder why things come to be in the first place, why they continue to exist, and what, if anything, will ultimately last.

Rooted in the fundamental experience of human dependency and vulnerability in the cosmos, both primitive religious creation myths and later philosophical speculation were concerned not only with the question of origins, but with the deeper issue of the unity, integrity and coherence of the cosmos. While at first glance the question about creation is the question about the origin of the world, we see that there is something much deeper at stake: the question of its ultimate meaning. Does reality make sense? Does it have a meaning, a purpose, an end, a future destiny? Let us consider what kind of answer biblical faith gives to these questions in its assertion that we are created by God.

The Creation Stories in Genesis

In the form it finally attained in exilic and post-exilic times, Genesis 1-11 provides a kind of prologue to the story of Israel's liberation and election by God. Looking backward from Israel's experience of God's action in creating and saving it as a people, and composed from different traditions, it presents God as the utterly transcendent Creator and Lord of the entire cosmos. The Yahwist tradition, commonly dated about the tenth century B.C.E., is the first to combine Israel's national epic with mythic stories about primeval history. It has its own particular vocabulary (including the use of the divine name "Yahweh"), a refined literary style and is characterized by well-developed theological reflection. The Priestly tradition, which dates from about the sixth century B.C.E., is attributed to the priests of Jerusalem. Its style is somewhat clipped, abstract and repetitive in comparison with the Yahwist tradition. It evidences a concern for detail and contains material greatly influenced by the community's life of worship. Both traditions, however, recognize the source, unity and meaning of the entire cosmos in its relationship with God. The Promise made to Abraham and the later Covenant with Israel are seen as intrinsically related to God's plan for all humanity. The powerful hand which led Israel out of Egypt is not merely one among many which appears one day, in one land, in the course of time. The power of that outstretched arm encompasses all time and places from the very beginning. It is the same arm which alone stretched out the heavens and made all things (Is 44:24). For Israel, absolutely no dimension of existence lies beyond the creating and liberating activity of God.

On one level, these stories offer explanations for different aspects of the human condition as we experience it, in the same way that the myths of Israel's neighbors did. But on a more fundamental level, they are concerned with the establishment of *rela-*

tionship. They are not meant to be reports about what actually happened "in the beginning," in the long ago past. They mean to speak about the God from whom and with whom the world now and always has life and future. This makes speaking about creation and creatureliness very different from speaking simply about existence or contingency. In fact, the biblical stories about creation are best understood as answers of faith, born of Israel's experience of God, to the basic and terrifying questions raised by our threatened, contingent existence. It is God and God alone whose hand holds back both Pharaoh's charioteers and the primal watery chaos, leading God's creatures to fullness of life and freedom. It is only in relationship with this God that the world and those who dwell in it can find real life, life that lasts (Deut 30:15-20).

God the Creator

If we turn to the opening chapters of Genesis, we find two different creation stories, each with something to say about the meaning of creation and creatureliness. The first is part of the Priestly tradition (from the sixth century B.C.E.) and the second is from the earlier Yahwist tradition (tenth century B.C.E.). According to the Priestly account, creation is understood to be the work of the Spirit/Word of God. God's Spirit is moving over the deep and God's mighty Word goes forth to create. In the Hebrew text, we find the word *bara'* used to denote this unique, divine creative activity. It is used later to refer to God's creation of a people in the Exodus out of Egypt and the Covenant on Sinai. In both cases we hear how God forms and gives reliability to what is dark, empty and chaotic. The Yahwist describes the Creator as one who planted a garden in Eden and brought forth human creatures to care for it.

The creation stories, therefore, are not talking about an almost magical act by which God makes something from nothing, like pulling a rabbit out of a hat or a bouquet of flowers from thin air. They focus, rather, on the divine power which forms, orders and sustains life.

Unlike many other mythical accounts of creation, Genesis does not offer us a picture of a great cosmic battle. There are no stupendous labors, no Herculean feats. God merely speaks and it is done. Because of the power of God's Word and because creation is the expression of God's desire and purpose, we can approach the world with confidence and hope in spite of the darkness and chaos which seem to threaten life. The world is reliable because it comes from God. It has a hope and a future because it is related to God.

It was later theology, appealing to 2 Macc 7:28, which said that God created the world "from nothing." This means that the world receives its entire being and constitutive identity from God, not from itself or from anything other than God. We are utterly dependent upon God. To be is to come to be *from* and with others, hence the "ex" in existence. Just as I owe my existence to other persons, the cosmos as a whole owes its being and life to an other, God. Moreover, God is not merely the one who started it all going, but the one who at every moment holds it in existence. The most basic dimension of reality is this relationship.

The expression "creation from nothing" points to the mystery of being and of our contingency, which occasionally registers in our feelings of wonder and awe. In the last analysis, there is no reason why there is anything at all, except God's gracious and free act. The cosmos of which we are a part is intended and desired by God. It is neither necessary nor arbitrary, a product of chance or chaos. The sovereign freedom with which God creates means that life is a gracious gift. I am invited to interpret my own experience of the indebtedness of existence as gift and grace.

But there is a second point which a bit of reflection on the notion of *creatio ex nihilo* reveals. In understanding reality as related to God in this radical way, Christian faith also believes that there is absolutely nothing in the nature of created reality which could be a constitutive principle of separation from or contradiction to God. While Paul's words to the Romans were written in another context, they are nonetheless beautifully appropriate here: "For I am sure that neither death, nor life, nor angels, nor principalities, nor things present, nor things to come, nor powers, nor height, nor depth, nor anything else in all creation, will be able to separate us from the love of God in Christ Jesus our Lord" (Rom 8:38f).

The Goodness of Creation

An attitude of realistic confidence and hope is rooted in the belief that because God created it and sustains it, the finite world is good. For God, and therefore presumably for us, it is good that there is something which is not God. The Priestly account of creation is like a litany. Over and over we hear a refrain which reminds us how good the creatures are found to be by their creator, until finally we read, "And God saw everything God had made, and behold, it was very good" (Gen 1:31).

Indeed, one of the first major theological tasks which faced the church in the second and third centuries was to defend its belief in the goodness of God's creation against the gnostics. One thing which the many diverse forms of gnosticism share is the conviction that the created world, precisely as material, could not really be the work of God, who is pure spirit. Whether the result of a primordial battle in the spiritual heavens, or the work of a divine-like demiurge, the world is bad. Redemption is conceived of as liberation from the created world and its evil materiality.

For biblical faith, on the contrary, the world is a good place in which to be. It is precisely where God places us and it is where God wishes to be in relationship with us. God does not wish to save us from the world. God wishes to save the world, and us humans who are a unique part of it, from the sin which threatens to destroy it and for which we are responsible. This is the whole point of the story about the "fall" of the first humans in Genesis 2-3. Faced with the reality of suffering and evil, the Yahwist tells us that human sin, not an evil or indifferent God, is to blame. This is how the Bible introduces us to the real story it has to tell, the story of how God has been at work saving the world.

Human Beings in God's Image and Likeness

Both creation stories emphasize the unique nature and position of human beings in creation. The Yahwist describes how the Lord God formed the "earth" creature and breathed into its nostrils to make it a living being. The Priestly account places humanity at the head of creation and gives us the concept which has proved most significant for Christianity's understanding of being human, the human being as image of God. "Let us make humanity in our image, after our likeness . . ." (Gen 1:26). Even though it is not developed in the OT, it seems taken for granted in the NT, and sets the stage for a specifically Christian understanding of God's saving act of recreation in which we are conformed to the image of God's Son (Rom 8:29).

First, a brief remark about the words image (*ṣelem*) and likeness (*dĕmût*). The first refers to a concrete, external form of representation, like a carved statue. Many scholars have suggested a background in the practice of the Egyptian pharoahs, who erected statues of themselves throughout their kingdom. In the mind-set of the time, it was thought that the Pharoah himself was actually present in these statues. They were representations that really "presented" him, made him present. As it stands, such a thought would be foreign to the OT understanding of God. But against this background, perhaps, we could take Gen 1:26 to mean that, although *only* an image of God (and not the divinity itself), humanity has been established as God's *representative* on earth in a unique way.

The term likeness refers more specifically to an internal relationship and similarity. Human beings are radically different from God but uniquely and intimately related to God, capable of personal relationship with God. According to the Priestly tradition, the human creature is defined primarily in relationship to God, not in terms of its relationship to the other types of creatures, the way we might place a particular animal in a specific phylum, genus and species. The human being is not merely *primus inter pares*, nor merely the highest among the animals. Some scholars[1] see an indication of the *difference* in the fact that sexual differentiation and subsequent procreation must be explicitly specified for humans in this text. One would assume this of animals, but not of an image of a God like Israel's, who transcends sexuality. It is this relationship with God which "defines" human nature and makes us different from all other creatures. It is also the foundation of the inviolable dignity of human life.

---

[1] For example, Phyllis A. Bird, " 'Male and Female He Created Them': Gen 1:27b in the Context of the Priestly Account of Creation," *Harvard Theological Review* 74/2 (1981), 147.

Let us now consider more exactly what this means. Three things stand out in the biblical text: (1) dominion over the rest of creation, (2) creation male and female and (3) the command to be fruitful and multiply.

Dominion Over the Earth: A Share in God's Power

The place of humanity at the head of creation seems to be stressed in the Priestly account. Does the language hint at this when it says that the human creatures are not "brought forth" from the waters or from the earth like the other animals? They are not merely God's works; they are created to be God's image. As such, they are given a share in God's dominion. In the OT, God's dominion is revealed in God's creating, sustaining activity in the world; it is a "divine milieu," both a "place" and a "power" for real life. For God, power is not some neutral potency, the ability to do just anything strongly. God's power is the strength, fullness and utter dependability of God's loving creation and creating love.

The dominion which humans have can only exist within, not outside or alongside of, God's dominion as the concrete expression of it. It can be nothing except the power and authority to care for, to nurture and to develop the whole world. There is nothing wrong with understanding God's creative desire and our God-given task as the "humanization" of the world as long as we understand that one of the things which makes us truly human is the distinctive ability to acknowledge, appreciate and delight in the reality of all other creatures as other, and to care for them. We are called to a cosmological and ecological mutuality which is founded on the goodness of creation and the delight which the Creator has in it. Therefore, to be God's image or representative on earth, to share in God's dominion, means that we receive a share in God's power *for* creation, not simply *over* creation. It does not give us a license to exploit it as we please. Human beings are accountable to the Creator for the world's well-being and wholeness. God alone is the Lord; the Lord alone is God (Deut 6:4).

Male and Female: The Mystery of the Other

Like other creation myths, the Priestly account addresses the reality of sexual differentiation (1:27). It is interesting that being created in the "image of God" is directly related by the text to being created "male and female." What does this suggest? It certainly cannot mean that God is both male and female. God's utter transcendence is central to Hebrew faith. God has no gender. God is neither gender specific nor gender composite. Precisely in this point, Israel's concept of God differed radically from that of its neighbors.

God's transcendence is forcefully expressed in the strict prohibition of graven images (Ex 20:4). This is all the more remarkable if we consider that God has made humans beings as God's *image*. Since we are created in God's image, the human, the personal, *is* a privileged, though analogical, way of thinking about God. Thus the Scriptures are filled with male and female images of God, and it is not only appropriate but important to use both, as long as we realize that such language is metaphorical. Unfortunately, the Judeo-Christian tradition, in its piety and theology, has deviated from this important truth. Even though the Scriptures themselves offer many examples of female images of God, God has been imaged and spoken of in predominantly male terms. Many claim that this has functioned to exalt the male and the "masculine" as divine, thus helping to create and legitimate an oppressive patriarchy. In order to help overcome this destructive exaggeration, we must learn to speak of God using female images (which is different from predicating of God culturally stereotyped "feminine" traits).

God is represented equally well (and with the same limitations!) by images of either sex. But since God is not a person in the ordinary sense of the word, perhaps God's very transcendence demands that we use both images. Gen 1:27 suggests that it is human *community,* both male and female, that most adequately images God as personal and relational, even if what it means to speak of God as person remains an incomprehensible mystery to us.

Precisely as God's image, we are challenged, especially in our public worship, both to recover traditional female images which have been lost or suppressed and to use our imaginations to create new ones. It is an important and difficult task, which demands tolerance, respect and love.

As Elizabeth Johnson has suggested, the creation of humanity in the image of God, male and female, brings the utter transcendence and incomprehensibility of God to unique expression.[2] On the other hand, it also speaks in an analogous way of the inviolable mystery, dignity and transcendence of the human creatures who image such a God. Sexual differentiation is a particularly clear example of our fundamental relationality and interdependence as human beings. I shall have more to say about this in the chapter on community. For now, I would only like to observe that the human person is not created simply as an individual and we cannot exist humanly as isolated individuals. From the first moment of life we are social beings who can only be human in communion with others. To be human means to be-in-relation, to be-with. Even more pointedly, it is something which is radically *from* others. It is essential that we recognize our real relationality, a truth often obscured by classical theology which, following Boethius, stressed the radical individuality of persons (the human being is an "individual substance of a rational nature"). This truth has also been forgotten by much modern thought since the Enlightenment, which stressed the freedom, rights and autonomy of the individual human subject. What and who *my* real "self" is, is a mystery which is constituted by the mystery of *others*.

This means that my humanity is something always profoundly greater, even other, than I am. Sexual differentiation highlights this. Scholars in a variety of disciplines have begun to take seriously what the poets and song writers have always told us: men and women seem to experience and understand reality in some remarkably different ways. Christian theology has tended to ignore this, treating human "nature" independently of its sexual concretization. While there is much that we can say about being human which is true about both men and women, perhaps we are only now beginning to realize that there is much which cannot be said quite so simply. Each of us, male or female, must

[2]Elizabeth A. Johnson, "The Incomprehensibility of God and the Image of God Male and Female," *Theological Studies* 45 (September 1984) 460.

realize the fact that there is *another* mode and experience of being human which is different from, and not reducible to, one's own. There is another way of being human which remains inaccessibly mysterious.

Therefore, no human being can claim to experience or understand the mystery of what it means to be human only from his or her humanity. The real humanity of each person, male or female, is something that points beyond itself to a real other. This is a paradox. Male and female are not simply accidental characteristics of human being; neither are they two different creatures. They are irreducibly different in one humanity.

This, it seems to me, expresses something of the mystery of God and about our relationship with God. The mystery of the sexually other human is a symbol of the absolute mystery of God's otherness and of our relatedness to and transcendence towards God as our final personal wholeness and fulfillment. Our humanity is essentially ecstatic, other-directed. We are whole and entire only in our relationships with others: both human others and with God, that divine Other.

Fruitfulness: Creativity and Future

Just as humanity male and female may share in and image the divine dominion (1:26) it is also the precondition for the divine command to "be fruitful and multiply" (1:28). Procreation is certainly a central way in which we share in and image God's creative power. (Creator comes from the Latin word which means to beget.) Of course, what is at issue here is the propagation of the species to ensure the "dominical" care of the earth, not the end of marriage or the normativity of monogamous heterosexual relationships.

Moreover, the command to be fruitful and multiply should not be understood narrowly, precisely because procreation is not an end in itself. The propagation of human life is the basic condition for the deeper fruitfulness and creativity of our lives. This story invites us to see a broader connection between God's creation and our creativity, and therefore, the theological importance of human labor. Human activity in all its forms is blessed with the possibility and responsibility of bearing fruit. In this way it is an image of God's creative act. Of course we do not literally create the world. It belongs to God alone to create, to bring into being out of the void and chaos. But the work of our hands can image God's creative act. Indeed, as we shall see in the next chapter, in gifting us with freedom, God has made us responsible for the shape which we give our lives and the world. In human beings, in a way far different from the fertility of the other creatures, the whole world is full of possibilities.

Ecology: Stewards of Creation

Western society has, to a large extent, lost a vital sense of connection to the earth. Especially since the Enlightenment, it has tended to see human reason and autonomy at the center of things. Since the Age of Discovery and the rapid accomplishments of science, this anthropocentrism has led to an ever more individualistic, utilitarian and exploitative attitude toward the world and its resources. It is true that the scientific advances of the last century, especially in physics, astronomy and space travel, have done something to rekindle a sense of awe in us and given us a more chastened appreciation of the infinitesimal size, and perhaps significance, of our planet in the universe. Nevertheless, these very advances have also tended to reinforce some of the worst traits of our basic technological and manipulative attitudes. We continue to put science to work in ways which threaten to destroy us.

Theologians like Sallie McFague remind us that we are living in an age when the threat of ecological and nuclear destruction are real and pervasive. Ironically, it is our very technological creativity and sophistication that have apparently given us the ability to destroy our human world. The consequences of these advances are making more and more people view the profound holistic sensibility of more "primitive" (!) peoples and times with greater respect. It is precisely in this context that we ought to listen to the biblical stories and look at their vision of the world.

In different ways, both creation stories stress that we are part of a unified, interrelated whole and have a special place in it. We have already focused on the Priestly account in some detail. Humanity as an image of God has a unique capability and responsibility for the well-being and future of the world. I would now like to turn to the Yahwist story of creation. It has a timely message for us and can challenge us to understand humanity in an ecological context. We are not merely beings who walk *on* the earth, we come from it and are truly a part of it.

The cultivation and care of creation is highlighted in the Yahwist account. I think it presents us with a more holistic view than the Priestly story. After a mist arises and waters the earth, God creates a man, forming him, as the name Adam indicates, out of the ground, making him alive with the divine breath (Gen 2:6-8).

Only then, with a human creature capable of tilling the ground (2:5) does God plant a garden and place the first human in it to tend it (2:15). How different from the Priestly account, in which the world in all its diversity is prepared for humanity and placed at its disposal! Like the Priestly writer, the Yahwist also indicates the special status of the human creature as the one who has the right to name the animals. But here the order and perspective are reversed. This text seems to say that God prepared for the abundant earth which was to be created, by first creating all that was necessary for its fruitfulness and well-being. Seen in this way, the earth is not simply created for humankind but humankind is created for the earth.

But it is not good that the human should be alone. In order that the first human might have a suitable partner, God created all of the other animals. While none was to be found, so the story continues, God created a woman from the rib of the man. Here at last is the partner suitable to help carry out the task of caring for the garden. The point here is not that the woman is subordinate to the man as a mere "helper" (the Hebrew word does not connote inferiority). Nor is loneliness the issue. The story takes place in a garden which must be cared for. The image of helper focuses not so much on the man, as it does on the garden, really the whole creation, which the human creatures are to till and for which they are responsible.

In God's plan, as the Yahwist understands it, the original relationship between humanity and the earth is one of responsible care. We are not merely the namers of the other creatures; we are not to be petty tyrants and manipulators. We must learn to see ourselves as gardeners, careful tenders of the earth, realizing that our mutual survival and development is at stake. The Yahwist image of gardening challenges false notions of God's dominion and the human patterns of both domination ("If God is in charge and has given me charge, then I can do what I please") and indifference ("If God is in charge, I don't have to worry; it doesn't matter what I do"). In human beings, the world becomes conscious of itself and able creatively and actively to choose its future. Human beings, by virtue of their uniquely transcendent capacity for relating to all the other creatures, are precisely the ones who have the enormous responsibility to choose a future which is really the future of the whole and not merely the advantage of a part. In *Sollicitudo Rei Socialis* (On Social Concern), Pope John Paul II emphasized the obligation we have to respect nature in order to ensure and just a human development of the cosmos.[3]

Today the hope that the world really does have a future is threatened more than ever. Christian hope for the world's future is based on God's faithful, sustaining, creative power. God's powerful Word, which brought the world into being is powerful enough to accomplish God's desire for the world's life. But both the OT and the NT witness the conviction that the life and fullness of the world will not be the predictable outcome of a process of evolution. And we moderns have become enlightened about the Enlightenment's belief in civilization and progress.

The life of the world is always a life that must be saved. It must be chosen intentionally, labored and sacrificed for. It is life that must be rescued from the many powers of death and destruction which threaten it. As Christians, we are part of a biblical tradition that asserts this explicitly of God. The world has a future because in Jesus Christ it has been chosen intentionally, labored and sacrificed for by God. God so loves the world (Jn 3:16). The key word here is *world*, not just me, certainly not just my soul, not even us or our collective souls. The Christian understanding of salvation must recover its inherent universality and inclusiveness. It is something which involves not just human beings, but the whole of creation.

[3]This encyclical commemorates the twentieth anniversary of Paul VI's social encyclical "Populorum Progressio" by taking up once again the important theme of authentic human development. See especially nrs. 27-45.

But it is important to consider for a moment what it really means to say that God wishes to save the world. If the reality of the world as a living, active, intentional and self-constituting whole is what God wishes to save, then it seems to me that God's saving activity is not something that happens alongside or instead of but *in* and *through* the world's activity, especially in and through human action. Therefore, the necessity that salvation come from God and the necessity that human beings take responsibility for the world's well-being are directly proportional. The greater our belief in salvation from God, the greater the obedience of faith to acknowledge our active responsibility for the world. God does not wish to save us from doing. God wishes to save us from all that would prevent us from doing!

According to the Yahwist narrative, humankind is intimately related to the Creator in a way that distinguishes it from the rest of God's creatures. This is not because human beings are enlivened by the breath of God (Gen 2:7), for God has breathed this breath into all the animals (Gen 7:22). Rather, the dignity of human beings is especially evident in their *partnership* with God in caring for creation. As tenders of the garden and stewards of creation, human beings are not mere underlings with a task to perform. If they are superior to the other creatures, it is because through them the creative, divine Spirit is present and active in a unique way. As a result, humans are more capable of and responsible for the well-being of the creation. Human beings are *from* God and the earth as well as *with* God *for* the earth. Thus the salvation which *God* desires and promises the world as its sure future is precisely what makes us acknowledge our *human* responsiblity for the world.

RELATED READING

Piet Schoonenberg, *God's World in the Making* (Pittsburgh: Duquesne University Press, 1964) presents a theology of the human world against the backdrop of evolution and the thought of Pierre Teilhard de Chardin. Michael Schmaus, *Dogma 2: God and Creation* (New York: Sheed & Ward, 1969) is a solid presentation of catholic doctrine. Jürgen Moltmann, *God in Creation: A*

New Theology of Creation and the Spirit of God (San Francisco: Harper and Row, 1985) approaches the subject with an ecological focus. Sallie McFague, *Models of God: Theology for an Ecological, Nuclear Age* (Philadelphia: Fortress Press, 1987) argues for new ways of imaging God and God's relationship to the world, as does Elizabeth A. Johnson, C.S.J., "The Incomprehensibility of God and the Image of God Male and Female" in *Theological Studies* 45 (September 1984), 441–65. David Cairns, *The Image of God in Man* (London: SCM Press, 1953) offers an historical, systematic survey of this important theological theme. Richard J. Clifford, S.J., "Genesis 1–3: Permission to Exploit Nature?" in *The Bible Today* 26 (May 1988), 133–35 clarifies the notion of God's dominion. This entire issue of *The Bible Today* focuses upon creation and the environment. Impulses for spirituality are given by Peter J. Schineller, S.J., "St Ignatius and Creation-Centered Spirituality" in *The Way* 29 (January 1989), 46–59.

2

The Gift of Human Freedom

In the last chapter we reflected upon the relationship between God's creating and human creativity. Created in God's image, men and women have been given a certain capacity and responsibility for what becomes of God's creation. For the Bible, God's sovereignty and human freedom go hand in hand. Human freedom, as a sharing in God's dominion, is grounded in God's own sovereignty, before which it is, therefore, ultimately responsible. God, not the human creature, is alone Lord of heaven and earth.

The mystery of creation is that there *can* be anything which is different from the infinite, boundless God. Christian faith understands the existence of the created world as the utterly free and gracious action of God. But according to biblical faith, God's Word does not call creation into some kind of merely factual existence, but to being-with-God. To be means to live with God, to participate in some way in God's life. When the Priestly writer tells us that God found all that God had made to be good, he is not referring to a moral quality or transcendental characteristic. He is speaking about the desire and delight that God has in relationship with creation. The smile of a mother holding her baby at the breast (Is 49:15) images God's delight in her creation: "It is good that you are here."

This means something quite astounding, something which we don't often take seriously. We are really free to be, free to be ourselves, different from God. The real freedom of the world is what God most intensely desires and is its greatest good. For, only in freedom can there be a real relationship of love in which each of the lovers takes delight in the mystery of the other.

The Covenant and the history of its fulfillment bring this to expression. This is a matter of the heart, of personal relationship. The Lord freed the people from slavery in Egypt and called them to abandon the false gods in whom there is no life. "I will be their God, and they shall be my people" (Jer 31:33). The sovereignty of the Lord over the cosmos is of secondary interest to Israel. What is of utmost importance is the fact that God has created a people and, like a husband speaking tenderly to his wife, has betrothed it to himself in faithfulness and steadfast love (Hosea 2). Creation and Covenant find their fulfillment in Jesus Christ, whose own person reveals what loving union between God and humanity really means, and in his Spirit, who is God's love poured out into our hearts (Rom 5:5). "Where the Spirit of the Lord is, there is freedom" (2 Cor 3:17).

Freedom is from God and for God. On its deepest level, it is the capacity and responsibility to be in loving relationship with God. It is the gift of love, the capacity for love and it finds its only true fulfillment in love.

Action, Desire and Choice

According to the Scriptures, in creating the world out of love in order to be its lover, God made a partner not a puppet. Meaningful talk about freedom is rooted in the experience of ourselves as real agents. If we were not capable of real action, if we were completely determined in our activity by forces over which we have no control, then it would not make sense to speak of freedom. What we do matters. If our actions were of no real consequence for ourselves and for the world, it would make no sense to speak of freedom.

We experience ourselves as agents; our action is characterized by intentionality and self-conscious choice. This is one of the key things which distinguishes us from the other creatures. Of course, not everything that we do, or all of the things happening while we act, are intentional. At this very moment, my cardiovascular system is working away. Since I am in good health, I am completely unaware of it most of the time. But as a result of it and many other processes, I am able to write this book. That *is* a matter of intention and choice. It is action in the strict sense of the term. And it is an experience of freedom.

Intentional agency is the basic experience of freedom. It cannot be demonstrated or disproved by neutral observation. On its simplest level, it presupposes real options and the ability to choose from among them what it is I decide to do. Of course, none of us has an unlimited range of options. We exist in a particular context and are determined to some extent by a whole matrix of relationships within it. For example, our genetic make-up is a given, as is the particular place and period of history in which we are born and live. From earliest childhood, we are all shaped in profound ways by familial and cultural forces about which we have no choice and over which we can exercise little control. They greatly influence the development of character and personality and evidently predispose us to certain kinds of interests and patterns of behavior. But our genetic, historical and cultural heredity does not determine in advance precisely what each of us will do in a given situation. Within such parameters, there is a wide range in which I can determine what I want to do and how I desire to live.

Our ordinary experience of freedom is in making such choices. Of course, some choices matter more than others. Students like the freedom to choose which of several questions they will answer on a final exam. All of us like the freedom to decide what clothes we are going to wear and what we are going to eat for lunch. But after student days have passed, exams do not seem so important. And decisions about food and clothing (so the birds of the air and the lilies of the field are meant to remind us) ought not to be the most important choices we make. Such things usually have little impact on the world or on ourselves as persons. The freedom to choose one's religion, country, home, profession, friends, and partner is considerably more basic to human life and dignity. The choices we make in these matters have a substantial and lasting impact.

The most important exercise of freedom, the most important choice we make in life, however, does not have to do merely with a particular thing or course of action. It has to do with our very selves. Freedom is the capacity to choose who I am going to become as a person. Life is not only a gift, it is a task as well. We are not merely objects thrown into existence, determined by others and outside influences. We are also subjects, responsible agents, *persons* who are challenged to say something, to do something, to become someone. At times, it can seem so overwhelming that we try to run away from it, either asking others to tell us what we should do or become or simply resigning to a fatalistic determinism. Freedom may be scary and unsettling at times, but we do have real choices to make about our lives. We cannot avoid them.

According to thinkers as diverse as Maurice Blondel, Karl Rahner, John Macmurray, and Eric Erikson, we are constituting our very selves through such choices. The values I choose to live by, how I deal with those aspects of myself and the world which I can't change, the profession I choose to dedicate most of my time and energy to, how I choose to treat my family and respond to the needs of those around me—all have a profoundly formative influence, both upon myself and upon others. The "real me" is not a predetermined statistic of heredity. Each of us is becoming a certain person in a process of self-actualization which takes place in the concrete choices he or she makes throughout life. Moreover, experience teaches that human action has an enduring, cumulative effect. The capacity for good and evil, for loving and hating grows *in action*. Our freedom itself is always on the line. Through our actions we are always becoming more or less human, more or less free to be in the life-giving relationships of love with others and with God for which we were created.

You are what you do? In a certain sense, yes. Of course, not everything we do is conscious and intentional. Not everything we consciously choose to do involves our deepest self and even if it does, there is always the possibility of a change of heart, for better or for worse. Consequently, no person can be reduced to a single action he or she performs, or even to the sum of all past actions. Nonetheless, many theologians correctly point out that in the important choices of life, taken together as a whole, each of us makes what might be called a *fundamental option* which forms the deepest core of our personal identity. It expresses our basic attitude toward self, others and God and informs subsequent particular decisions we make. Thus, it is clear that for real human growth in freedom, attention to the basic direction and underly-

ing attitude which is taking shape in my life is much more important than any particular choice or action in itself. For precisely
in my free responses, I am deciding *to be* in a particular way and,
therefore, to become a certain person. We see, therefore, that beyond the level of choice among options, human freedom is the
capacity and responsibility for *self-determination*.

While freedom certainly entails the ability to change one's mind
or to have a real change of heart, its goal is not infinite options
or endless revision. As a matter of fact, change just for the sake
of change is often a sign of immaturity or great unfreedom. In
many respects, we are freest when, no longer torn in different
directions by a multitude of possibilities, we can at last surrender
to one of them whole-heartedly. We have moved from a superfi-
cial level of freedom as the ability to change constantly to the
depth dimension of freedom as the ability to "get it all together,"
to reach some kind of personal wholeness and integral identity
which lasts. Freedom is really the capacity finally to commit oneself, to "become somebody," not to be somebody different every
day. As the great catholic theologian Karl Rahner put it, freedom is the capacity to dispose finally of oneself, to make oneself
once and for all.[1] This is the central project of our adult lives.

At any given moment in life, we stand between a past already
determined by the choices we have made and an undetermined
future of different possibilities. The very existence of options and
the importance of choosing make us aware of deeper questions:
What do I really want? What am I hoping to accomplish? Who
do I wish finally to become? These are the questions of *desire*
and they are fundamental to our understanding of freedom. Desire
is the affective side of freedom. Freedom is the capacity to desire.

What is it that we most deeply desire? I suppose the most basic
answer is "life." Life is found only in relationships with others.
To be alone is to die. Our basic desire for life and fulfillment is
what leads us outside of ourselves. Freedom is the capacity for
such self-transcendence, the power to reach out beyond ourselves.
We desire to know about other things and persons and to be in
life-giving relationships of love with them. If we pay attention
to these experiences, we can see that our desire is open-ended,

[1]Karl Rahner, *Foundations of Christian Faith* (New York: Seabury, 1978) 96.

unbounded. It never comes to rest. Learning and loving always seem to leave us restless, hungry for more. Our desire for life is unrestricted; no single object or person completely satisfies it. Moreover, our experiences of life and love, as deep and life-giving as they might be, are all fragile, often damaged, sometimes destroyed by human failures and ultimately threatened by death itself. Throughout our lives, the desire which drives us in our interaction with other people and things is looking for life and love which is full and lasting. This is what Augustine meant when he said that our hearts will never come to rest until they rest in God. What we most deeply desire is God. God alone is life and love in unsurpassable fullness.

But can the infinite God really be the fulfillment of human beings, who as finite creatures remain radically different from God? Is the divine life a real goal and end which can be reached, or does God remain a silent, ever-receding and unattainable horizon? Christian faith proclaims that in Jesus Christ, God has drawn near, become human. The infinite capacity of human "nature" is revealed definitively and irrevocably in the humanity of Jesus, far beyond all notions of intimacy and partnership which we found in the stories of Genesis. Created human freedom is ultimately a real capacity for God. Its unrestricted openness is truly an image of and capacity for God's infinity; its never-ending desire made for eternal life and love. If we are really capable of being one with God, then nothing else but loving union with God will make us whole and entire. Only God can be the "object" of a complete, unconditional, final, and finally fulfilling choice.

This is what human freedom is finally for. This is where human freedom comes to its fulfillment. But how do we "choose" God, how do we enter more fully into God's love? God does not appear on the scene as one distinct "object" among many others to be chosen and loved. God's presence is *mediated*. The fundamental and abiding medium of our real relationship with God is this world, God's beloved creation. The only mode we have of experiencing God, of relating with God, of accepting God in love or turning from God in selfishness, is in terms of this world and our action in it. In all that we do, we are at least implicitly taking a stand with respect to God and God's offer of life.

Edith Stein, a Carmelite philosopher who was gassed by the

Nazis, once said that those who search for the truth are looking for God whether they know it or not. Modifying this slightly we could say that whenever we really love this world or any part of it, truly and honestly for what it really is; whenever we respect it, hope for it, care for it; whenever we attend to the needs of the least of our brothers and sisters—we are meeting and loving God, whether we realize it or not. This seems to be the message of Matthew 25, especially as we ponder the surprise expressed by the just, who did the loving, human, everyday things, without experiencing them explicitly in a religious way. This is why Karl Rahner and Piet Schoonenberg stress that the love of God and the love of neighbor are really one. Only love can make us truly free and bring us the wholeness we call salvation.

In Jesus Christ, and in the Kingdom which he preached, Christians may see the freedom to which they are called. None of the apostles preached this more passionately than Paul, who exhorted the Galatians to hold fast to the freedom which was theirs in Christ, a freedom which builds community and enables loving, creative service (5:13). He makes it clear that true freedom is not merely freedom *from*; it is a freedom *for*. It is not merely the autonomy of the Enlightenment. It goes far beyond the "rights" of the individual in modern society. It is a freedom for others, a freedom for service, a freedom for love. It is the freedom to be with and for the others, the freedom which is the heart of true community.

This is what God wills; this is all God desires. It sums up the Law. In everything else God has truly made us free. Can we really believe that Christ has set us free *for freedom* (Gal 5:1), with no other "hidden agenda," no new set of rules and regulations?! God wishes us the real freedom to become lovers and so enter into the fullness of life. I do not think it matters much to God how exactly each of us desires to do that. Augustine put it beautifully: "Love and do what you wish."

It is clear that our freedom is itself something which needs to be set free. In some manner, each of us suffers from the imprisoning effects of sin in the world. All of us are to some extent caught up in ourselves, unable to reach out freely to others. It is hard to love, especially when it requires sacrifice and promises no romantic payoff. Disordered affections or addictions often frustrate or prevent loving relationships. It is not always easy to get in touch with the deepest desires of our hearts, to know what I really want to do or become. In this context, it is easy to understand why the NT almost always speaks about freedom as a grace of God, the gift of the Spirit which overcomes the selfishness and slavery of sin. We shall consider this in greater detail in subsequent chapters.

In the end, therefore, freedom does not refer so much to the rights of private, individual human beings, as it does to the foundation of a living communion of love. Freedom is the capacity and responsibility for human community and divine communion. This leads us to the theme of the next chapter.

RELATED READINGS

Bernard Häring, *Free and Faithful in Christ: Moral Theology for Clergy and Laity 1: General Moral Theology* (New York: Seabury Press, 1978) has an excellent treatment of freedom, responsibility and fundamental option. Karl Rahner's key essay is "Theology of Freedom" in *Theological Investigations 6* (New York: Seabury Press, 1974), 178–96. John Macmurray, *The Self as Agent* (Atlantic Highlands, N.J.: Humanities Press, 1978) presents a philosophy of freedom and action. It is a pity that this excellent book, originally delivered in 1953 as the Gifford Lectures at the University of Glasgow, is out of print.

3

The Individual in Community

"No man is an island," wrote John Donne many years ago. Of course this is obviously true on the physiological level. But on the personal level, judging from the experience of many modern men and women, such a statement would seem to express a fragile hope for an ideal future rather than a real description of today. In this chapter, I want to consider community and its significance for an authentic Christian understanding of human persons. This is especially important, given the great emphasis on the individual person which has characterized much of Western philosophical, religious and political thought. If, as Walter Kasper claims, the notion of the ultimate worth of the individual person came into the world with Christianity, it needs to be admitted that many countries where Christianity has flourished evidence an individualism and competitiveness which has nothing to do with the Gospel. Personal freedom often seems to mean little more than "the right to do whatever one wants" (not always with the proviso, "as long as it doesn't hurt anyone else"). For the individual to count, he or she must somehow be better than the others. Competition, not cooperation, is the model. Winners exist at the expense of losers. Even in religious matters, the stress on saving one's soul seems rather individualistic.

Being-in-Relation

The purpose of these reflections is to show that being human is essentially interpersonal and communal. The dignity of the human person as an individual is to be understood in the context of community. The freedom of each individual is itself a thoroughly social reality. The self-actualization which we spoke of in the preceding chapter necessarily and intrinsically involves the development of other persons and the world as a whole.

I know of no one recently who has developed this more persuasively than the Scottish philosopher John Macmurray did in the Gifford Lectures of 1953–4 entitled *The Form of the Personal.* What follows is greatly indebted to him. He suggests that the basic "unit" or "form" of the personal is not the solitary "I" but the "You and I."[1] In a certain sense, being an individual self is something derivative, not only biologically, but also psychologically. Our original and primary consciousness is the experience of the mother-child relationship in its unity. The child discovers itself as a self only in a progressive differentiation of this original unity. The child grows to be aware of itself as the one who is different from and in relation with, first with its mother and then other persons in a larger matrix of other relationships. These form a community of which the child is an individual member.

The absolute importance of this relationality is seen when we reflect on the fact that while the human being may be the most developed animal, it is certainly one of the most vulnerable at birth and during the first years of its life. Its survival depends completely upon the conscious, continuous and self-sacrificing care of others who provide food, clothing, shelter as well as stroking and smiling attention. The cries of the baby remind us that the earliest and abiding experience of personal reality is that I need you to be and become myself. The adult may in many ways become "self-sufficient" but will become ever more aware of the fact that life is not something which comes from one's own self, but from others.

Experience teaches us, moreover, that the other, precisely as personal, cannot be forced to give me what I need or believe I need. The paradox of human being as interpersonal is that what we truly need to live and to become self-actualized is something

---

[1]John Macmurray, *Persons in Relation* (Atlantic Highlands, NJ: Humanities Press, 1979) 61.

which I must receive as a freely bestowed gift from others. To be, and to be a self, is a gift, it is the fundamental *grace*. I cannot live and become myself unless there is an other who desires it and effectively communicates it to me. We are that dependent upon each other!

The basic good of life, therefore, is of its very nature something which is the life of the whole creation. The life of individual persons is something which is part of and relative to the whole. This is not to say that the value of human life is a question of arithmetic, that the life of an individual person is worth less than the welfare of the whole, or that a group, be it family, community, state or nation, may view individual members as expendable. It means that the life of each individual *is* the life of the whole and vice-versa. Whether I want to admit it or not, what I think of as *my* life is never just mine. And it cannot reach its full development unless I also intend the full development of the whole, of which it is a part. Thus, the final good of each and every individual human person must be seen as the mutual interrelationship of persons in a community which includes all persons, in which each cares for the others and for the nonpersonal creatures placed in their care.

It is a long journey from the beginning of our relationality, in which we are utterly dependent on others, to a community of equality and mutuality. We often treat people as things, rather than as other persons like ourselves. We see them only as means to an end, which may be my own growth or happiness. But as the real capacity to love develops, it brings with it its own sense of creative, caring power and responsibility. On its most basic level, conscience is the recognition that living and loving are coextensive. Moral responsibility is the recognition that true human community is a challenge and a task, not simply a given. It must be intentionally chosen.

This is what makes us different from other animals which exhibit what may be called herd instinct, or insects like ants and bees which seem to exhibit society-like structures. For us humans, the matrix of interpersonal relationships is not just a factual, instinctual given. It is not merely organic or evolutionary. It is personal and therefore intentional. Human community must be desired, chosen, created and worked for.

Such community can only come about when human persons relate to each other *personally*, and that means in relationships based upon equality, mutuality and affection. Community is only real as the action of human persons entering into communion with one another. It may sound silly to put it this way. But it is as simple and as difficult as that. Today the word "community" is often used, and in my opinion carelessly used, to describe different groupings in our society. Real community, however, is not based merely on a shared objective or common purpose. An interest group is not necessarily a real community. Communities are not automatically or necessarily formed because of gender, sexual orientation, occupation, talent or even common oppression. Of course, anything that persons share can be a fertile garden for real community to grow. But real community is not just the sharing of a common trait, interest or experience. It is the desire to share one's own self in love. It is based on the positive bonding of mutual affection. This is the difference between society and true community.

For community to be full, it must be inclusive. It must continue and develop the self-transcendence and other-relatedness that characterizes each one of us as a human being. The end toward which such growth tends is a community without limit in which all persons are free to become fully active in love.

Seen in this light, the challenge of community is the overcoming of all that impedes love. This is another way of speaking about freedom, justice and mercy. Practically speaking, it means the overcoming of fear and the selfish, private individualism which fear usually breeds. The more I am dominated by fear, the more likely it is that I relate to people as things, using them, manipulating them, always trying to take what can only really be freely given. And, paradoxically, the fearful person is likely to try to relate to things as if they were persons, seeking in them the kind of acknowledgment, affirmation, aggrandizement that can only be given personally in love.

The challenge of community requires that the relatively egocentric and competitive aspects which appear in human development be ordered with respect to the positive motivation of love which is attentive not only to its own needs but to the needs, hopes and dreams of others.

Above all, community requires the ability to forgive where, through human failure or betrayal, relationships of mutual trust, respect and love have been damaged.

Community and communion are the central issues of *religion*. The etymology of the word "religion," though somewhat obscure and disputed, is nonetheless highly suggestive. Religion concerns what binds us together, what we bind ourselves to, what we must bind ourselves to again and again if we are to live. The concerns of community are properly religious. In a wide variety of ways, religions seek to express this consciousness of community and its connection with the hope for salvation as the fullness and oneness of life.

The Biblical Vision

Such community is at the heart of biblical faith. It comes to expression in the central biblical themes of creation and Covenant. At the center is the liberation from Egypt, which is the creation of a people from the chaos of enslaved nomads, a true community with a real life and a real future, but only together with God. With ruthless honesty, the OT reflects on the journey of this people. Their failure to embrace such communion with God and community with one another is the failure of men and women of all times. In a particularly dramatic way, the Yahwist narrative in Genesis 2–12 sees this failure at humankind's very beginnings. After the intimate communion between the first humans and their Creator is disrupted, we read of an alarming disintegration of human community. Adam and Eve blame one another, Cain kills his brother Abel and Cain's descendent Lamech brags about his own murderous act. The extent of this disintegration becomes manifest in the deathly chaos of the flood. Even after a new creation and the covenant with Noah, we see the deadly fruit of the pride which has infected humanity. When men and women are interested only in making a name for themselves, the inevitable result is Babel, the breakdown of communication and the destruction of community. This, after all, was the temptation and sin of Adam. In the enormous cities of today, it is not difficult to be touched by the Yahwist's pessimism, which often seems to view cities and their so-called civilization as the inheritance of Cain.

The end of this horrible primeval history, however, is not the disintegration of Babel, but the call of Abraham. The Lord graciously promises to restore community by making Abraham a great nation. In stark contrast to Babel, where the prideful, self-centered ploy to "make a name" brought only destruction, here God promises to make Abraham's name great, a blessing for all the families of earth (Gen 12:1-3).

Throughout Israel's history, powerful images appear on the lips of the prophets, which remind the people who they are, who God is and what they are called to become: the community of God's people. The Law of life is rediscovered only to be broken. Even kings like David and Solomon cannot establish such community or guarantee peace and justice. And so the people long and look for the promised Messiah. The Kingdom of God, which is pictured in all its beauty on God's Holy Mountain, becomes an image of their hope for such a future as promised and established by God.

In the NT, Jesus appears preaching the coming of God's Kingdom. Those who believed in him recognized that he was no mere prophet pointing to a Kingdom yet to come. In the light of his death and resurrection, they realized that the Kingdom he spoke of had really drawn near. It had broken into this world by breaking the stronghold of sin, death and the fear they breed. They recognized it in Jesus' message and ministry. His words provoked a more radical answer to the questions "Who is my neighbor?" and "Who are my brothers and sisters?". His deeds restored the poor and marginalized to life in the community. The Gospel of Matthew, in the Sermon on the Mount and the healings which surround it, and the Acts of the Apostles, in the descriptions of the earliest communities, give us particularly vivid portraits of how this Kingdom could take real form in the life of the community.

Paul spoke of the new creation which was the Spirit's work and tirelessly called his fledgling churches to enter fully into communion with Christ, the New Adam, in the community of believers, his Body, the Church. The gifts of the Spirit are not for private persons but for the common good of the whole body. "For just as the body is one and has many members, and all the members of the body, though many, are one body, so it is with Christ"

(1 Cor 12:12). Apart from the body, a member is only a dead organ.

The God of the Law and the Prophets, the God of Jesus Christ, is the one whose creating and redeeming action transforms this world into God's Kingdom and calls all men and women to the freedom and divine fullness of life in this Kingdom by entering into free, forgiving and loving relationships in human community.

The Church: Sacrament of Communion and Community

Many theologians have pointed out how central the notion of community is in the ecclesiology of Vatican II. Both *Lumen Gentium* and *Gaudium et Spes* focus on the church as the People of God and stress the communitarian nature of human life and eternal salvation. Isolated and alone, human persons cannot develop their gifts or attain their destiny. God did not create human beings for life in isolation, but for the formation of social unity (GS 32). So also it pleased God to make men and women "holy and save them not merely as individuals, without any mutual bonds, but by making them into a single people" (LG 9), a people which embraces all men and women as one, a kind of "universal community" (GS 9), the "Family of God" (GS 32).

To this end, the church as community understands itself as a "kind of sacrament or sign of intimate union with God, and of the unity of all humankind" (LG 1). Together with the peoples of the world who "try harder every day to bring about a kind of universal community" (GS 9), the church is an "instrument for the achievement of such union and unity" (LG 1). Ultimately, it understands itself as an instrument, not merely in the hands of human believers, but in the "hands of God" (as Irenaeus called them), the Son and the Spirit. It is a living witness to the divine trinitarian love which is the origin, ground and final goal of human community.

Human community in communion with God: this expresses both the nature and the mission of the church. Since Vatican II, important documents like Paul VI's *Populorum Progressio* (1967), the American Bishops' pastoral letter, *Economic Justice for All: Catholic Social Teaching and the U. S. Economy* (1986) and John Paul II's *Sollicitudo Rei Socialis* (1988) have emphasized that the development and perfection of the world as a universal community of love is not simply a secondary dimension of the church's mission, but its very center. God's saving action is directed precisely toward the establishment of true human community. Therefore the church seeks to contribute to the wider application of justice and charity in the world by preaching the truth of the Gospel and shedding light on all areas of human activity (GS 76). The way of love is open for all and God gives the assurance that the effort to establish a universal communion of sisters and brothers will not be a hopeless one (GS 38). God wishes to bring the life-giving love and justice of the Kingdom to the world now, not simply in an "after" life. Faith in the power of God's love to transform this earth is what gives believers the courage and confidence to dedicate themselves to the service of God's earth in the work of the Kingdom.

RELATED READINGS

John Macmurray, *Persons in Relation* (Atlantic Highlands, NJ: Humanities Press, 1979), the second part of *The Form of the Personal*, argues that the personal self is constituted by its relation to others, and that human being is, therefore, radically communal. A brilliant book well worth tracking down. William A. Barry, S.J., "What Makes a Group a Community" in *Human Development* 8 (Winter 1987), 6–11, is an excellent development of Macmurray's notion of community in connection with religious life. Walter Kasper, *Theology and Church* (New York: Crossroad, 1989) has an excellent chapter on the church as communion. Karl Rahner, "Reflections on the Unity of the Love of Neighbor and the Love of God" in *Theological Investigations 6* (New York: Seabury Press, 1974), 231–49 establishes the theological connection between human community and communion with God.

4

Humanity: Male and Female

Insasmuch as the social, political, cultural and religious fabric of societies within the Judeo-Christian tradition has been virtually determined by men for thousands of years, we should have a good dose of suspicion about what we take for granted as "human nature." All too often, the voices of women have been silenced. Today, thankfully, we can hear new voices and are slowly learning to listen. It is absolutely necessary. The fact of sexual differentiation itself should remind us that no one, male or female, can ever claim to have plumbed the depth of human experience. There is another mode of being human which is different from mine, perhaps radically different, and just as human.

While the actions and message of Jesus did much to liberate women, the cultural, philosophical and even biblical influences which most deeply shaped theology and church life viewed women as inferior to men, often evil and even less than human. It seems far more important, therefore, to focus on this basic issue than the "traditional" topics surrounding the sexes, marriage and sexual morality. Until problems on this fundamental level are addressed, treatment of more specialized questions will remain compromised. Pondering the mystery of the real differentiation of the sexes, an authentic Christian anthropology must emphasize the dignity, freedom, equality and mutuality of men and women.

The Scriptures

Clearly, the Scriptures are a key source for a Christian under-standing of man, woman and sexuality. They cannot be ap-proached, however, as a source of timeless, objective truths. The composition, interpretation and use of Scripture depends on the particular historical context. Believers are often aware of world views and particular assumptions which they can no longer share with the biblical writers. This does not, in the catholic view, call into question the authority of the Scriptures as God's revelation. The point is that the truth of revelation must not be confused with the various cultural, philosophical, religious and scientific presup-positions of the biblical writers. The NT writings themselves offer proof by example of change and development. Moreover, the his-tory of exegesis shows that the biblical texts, together with in-sights gained from other sources, have a remarkably enduring, critical power. The Bible is full of *self*-critical voices as well!

I would like to focus on the OT creation stories which we have already considered in the chapter on creation. Because they un-derlie the basic NT attitudes and assertions about the sexes, I will turn only briefly to the NT, pointing out some of the significant changes we can observe.

It seems fairly clear to me that the Priestly and Yahwist writers are part of patriarchal societies and it is natural that their stories are told from a corresponding perspective. Nonetheless, as recent studies have shown, the texts themselves provide many challenges to this androcentrism and offer valuable insights for understand-ing the mystery of human being, male and female.

We have already seen that in the view of Genesis 1 and 2, God has created humanity male and female in God's image. Sexuality is good. Whatever the assumptions of the author may have been, Gen 1:26-28 has no hint of male-female hierarchy. What is cen-tral is the human-divine hierarchy. God shares God's dominion with humanity male *and* female in order that they might actively image this dominion in and over creation. Created "male and fe-male" in God's image, the sexes may be seen as equal in dignity and authority. Neither does the story of the creation of the woman from the rib of the first "man" in Genesis 2 justify such a hier-archy. As Lisa Sowle Cahill has pointed out, the "man" is made from the dust but is not inferior to it.[1] More likely the point is the origin of both male and female from one flesh (2:23), something which the Yahwist clearly relates to marriage (2:24), with the unusual twist that the "man" leaves his family to cling to his wife. Even the designation of the woman as "helper" to the "man" is not an indication of inferior status but of partnership in the care of creation. The Yahwist, more than the Priestly writer, seems to stress that sexuality serves the perpetuation of the human race, which in turn is directed toward human stewardship of God's creation. The well-being of humanity male and female is directly tied to the common good of all creation.

According to Genesis 3, this initial, divinely willed equality and mutuality is destroyed by human sin. Its terrible consequences, alienation and hierarchy between the sexes, the disruption of the harmony of creation, suffering and death, are the result of sin, a perversion of God's plan for creation. Equality and partnership between the sexes and human dominion of creation degenerate into domination and exploitation.

These traditions, together with other cultural and political influences, form the basis of different NT perspectives on sexuality. Paul is obviously an important example, particularly since his views have had an enormous impact on subsequent theology and church life. In 1 Corinthians 11, addressing certain liturgical problems, he calls for the subordination of women in the order of worship in the context of a theology of "headship" which is based on Genesis. Does this imply a strict hierarchy? It would seem to, although verses 11-12 make the point that "in the Lord woman is not independent of man nor man of woman . . . all things are from God". Then again there is the instruction in chapter 14, possibly an interpolation, that in church, women are not "permitted to speak, but should be subordinate, even as the law says" (14:34). On the other hand, in Galatians, where Paul brings his Gospel of freedom from the Law in the Spirit to its most forceful expression, he writes that for the baptized, there is neither Jew nor Greek, slave nor free, male nor female. All are "one in Christ Jesus" (3:28).

---

[1] Lisa Sowle Cahill, *Between the Sexes: Foundations for a Christian Ethics of Sexuality* (Philadelphia: Fortress Press, 1985) 54f.

Indeed, many scholars point out that both Paul and the Gospels reflect how subversive the life and teaching of Jesus were toward the patriarchal structures in Jewish and Gentile cultures of the time. Paul's provision for divorce is a case in point. Conversion of individual women in families was also threatening to existing familial custom and social order. Noteworthy is the independence and activity of many women in the early church, in nearly every form of ministry. Doubtless, this has its roots in the very ministry of Jesus. Women were among his closest friends and truest disciples. They were the first witnesses to the resurrection. The stories about the Samaritan woman in John 4 and the Syrophoenician woman in Mark 7 reveal just how unusual and open his relationships with women were, as startling as those with sinners and tax-collectors. Positive images of women fill his parables. It is hard to underestimate the critical impact of all this upon Jesus' contemporaries and the succeeding generations.

It seems clear to me, therefore, that despite the historical context in which the Scriptures are embedded and by which they are limited, the Scriptures continue to provide a vital and critical perspective.

Toward a Renewed Christian Anthropology

Scholars in many fields are calling our attention to differences between the sexes to which we were previously blind. Are they different enough to require dual anthropologies? Scripture, experience and current research seem to say No. Scripture affirms that human nature is shared. Humanity is one nature which subsists in two distinct modes, male and female. Each is fully human but the full humanity of each is a relational mystery which necessarily includes the other in some way. Each is fully human but neither is exhaustively human. We may speak of human "nature" or of the human "condition," but we must be careful that both men and women are speaking. Moreover, as Valerie Saiving pointed out years ago, Christian faith and theology rightly consider all human beings as finite, embodied, spiritual, free, sinful, graced and redeemed but how that is experienced and what it means for women may be quite different than for men. In many societies and cultures, pride and aggressive self-assertion may be a good paradigm of sin for men, whereas women may be tempted to self-deprecation and submission.

Sex and Gender Roles

Many important issues concerning men and women, both in the church and in society at large, raise the fundamental question about the relation between sex, gender and role. It is the subject of on-going research in the areas of biology, psychology, sociology and anthropology. Sex (male or female) is a biological fact. Gender, as I understand it, refers to a complex process of socialization and is far more fluid. It involves what it *means* in a given context to be male or female, what counts as "masculine" or "feminine." This is where the real issues of sexual and gender identity are crucial and complicated. While the difference between male and female is (thus far!) a question of universal and constant biological factors, what is considered to be "masculine" or "feminine" is neither universal nor constant. While recent studies suggest interesting cognitive and emotional differences between the sexes (men, for example, are more spatial, "right side" of the brain; women more verbal, "left-side"), it would be a mistake to establish precise and rigid categories here. And there is no justification to conclude that there are certain roles (beyond the obvious procreative ones) which are exclusively proper to one sex or the other. Neither theory nor empirical data supports rigid biological determinism. What, except the reenforcement of possibly sexist convention, is accomplished by referring to certain traits or roles as characteristically "masculine" or "feminine"?

For biblical faith, freedom is the central characteristic of human nature. The essence of this freedom is the capacity and responsibility for self-determination in community with other persons and with God. Thus, while each of us is to some extent determined by a number of factors (physical, biological, cultural and so on), our human "nature" is to a great extent something which God has empowered us to freely imagine, create and shape. This open-endedness or transcendence of human beings touches our sexuality as well. Beyond the merely biological, what it means to become a man or a woman, "masculine" or "feminine," is and remains a mystery, something open-ended, full of possibilities.

Experience teaches that sexual, gender and role identity have always been shaped by powerful human forces, societal, cultural and religious. Today we are more aware of this fact. Realizing that these realities are, to a large extent, our creations and not divinely established orders, we must assume responsibility for them, adopt a critical attitude toward them and seek to ensure that humanity male and female reflects the freedom, equality, dignity and mutuality which *are* divinely given and willed. In so doing, we must remember that no one has the authority to determine what it means to be a "manly" man or a "womanly" woman. Masculinity and femininity, important dimensions of our real, concrete way of being human persons, are precisely *human*, and therefore, part of a mysterious God-given realm of freedom, imagination and possibility.

Sexuality and Human Relationships

I would like to close this chapter with a few reflections on the role of sexuality in being and becoming human. They are necessarily brief, for to do more than that would involve developing an entire sexual morality. We have seen how Christian faith, basing itself on biblical traditions, values the difference of the sexes. Together, in relationships of freedom, equality, dignity and mutuality, men and women are called to creative partnership with God as stewards of creation. This includes, but is much broader than, procreation and survival of the species. It involves not only our personal relationships, but the importance of human labor and the development of the world.

It would seem that marriage and family life is the form in which the biblical call to such partnership and stewardship will be actualized for most men and women, but it is not the only one. Sexuality, human development and productive engagement in the world are basic issues for single persons and for gays and lesbians as well. Here, as in many other areas, our perspectives and experiences may vary greatly with those of the biblical writers. Moral theologians are faced with a crucial and extremely difficult task as they attempt to articulate how the Bible can function as a norm for concrete decision making in sexual matters. Obviously listening to the voices of experience is absolutely essential.

Although the creation stories of Genesis are centered upon a man and a woman, they remind us of the fundamental blessing and challenge shared by all persons: the gift and call not to be alone, to be with and for others and to contribute to the development of the world. Here is where we can see the power and grace of sexuality. In the experience of erotic desire, our other-directedness and interdependence find powerful expression. We are drawn out of ourselves and caught up in the other person. We are then faced with the challenge of real loving. Male or female, homosexual or heterosexual, single, married or celibate, the real test is whether or not we desire and love others in their real otherness, or whether we only want to take possession of them or try to make them extensions of ourselves. Sex is not the only way to express and nurture loving union, but it is one of the most intimate and powerful. Like other aspects of our lives, however, it can also be thoughtless and even exploitative. It is one of the most basic powers in human existence of liberation or domination, fulfillment or alienation, grace or sin.

Some may wonder what sex and erotic love have to do with the great commandment of love, which is at the heart of the Judeo-Christian tradition? In the NT, such love is called *agape* and refers directly to our love for God and neighbor (Mt 22:34-40). Many writers have viewed *agape* as the selfless, disinterested, and above all, dispassionate charity which Christians are supposed to have for others. Of course that usually made it the clear opposite of *eros*, sexual love, which was seen as self-directed, possessive and passionate. I think such a view is wrong.

Richard Gula, a catholic moral theologian, has suggested that "hospitality" conveys the sense of *agape*.[2] The heart of hospitality is being caught up in the feelings and needs of the other. Above all, it depends on attentiveness. It is not merely disinterested etiquette. In the Bible, hospitality involves the deeply affective dimensions of family, friendship and reverence. In the present context, this might remind us that everything about us as humans is ultimately directed towards and finds fulfillment in others, in the human community, and finally in God. *Eros* and *agape* are

---

[2]Richard M. Gula, *Reason Informed by Faith: Foundations of Catholic Morality* (New York: Paulist Press, 1989) 179f.

not opposed. Sexual love is called to be an expression of delight in the other, desire for the other and self-gift to the other. Delight, desire and self-gift come to unique expression in the vulnerable, hope-filled play and pleasure of making love. However, sex rarely creates or communicates these things *ex nihilo*. It will be authentic and satisfying, a grace and blessing, in the measure that it expresses and celebrates the delight, desire and self-gift that occur in the many different dimensions and events of everyday life. And it will reveal its saving, liberating power in the measure that the partners find their interest, attentiveness and commitment to the larger human community nourished and strengthened.

RELATED READINGS

One of the most helpful books I have read is Lisa Sowle Cahill, *Between the Sexes: Foundations for a Christian Ethics of Sexuality* (Philadelphia: Fortress Press, 1985). An excellent critical survey of recent developments in feminist theology, including a chapter on theological anthropology, and an excellent bibliography, is Anne E. Carr, *Transforming Grace: Christian Tradition and Women's Experience* (San Francisco: Harper and Row, 1988). Judith Plaskow, *Sex, Sin and Grace: Women's Experience and the Theologies of Reinhold Niebuhr and Paul Tillich* (Washington: University Press of America, 1980) is also very good. The groundbreaking article of Valerie Saiving, "The Human Condition: A Feminist View" in *The Journal of Religion* 40 (April 1960), 100–12, is still very illuminating.

5

Body and Soul

When Vatican II teaches that the human person "though made of body and soul. . .is one" (GS 14), it reiterates traditional church teaching which is quite familiar to most believers. Popular catechisms, more specialized theology books and, above all, the daily prayers of the church's liturgy, have taught us to think of the human being in terms of the pair "body and soul." Most people have probably not spent much time wondering exactly what these terms refer to. After all, it seems fairly obvious what the body is. I can see it, touch it, probe it, embrace it. It is what people look at when I say "Here I am." Each of us has one. And, as most of us were taught, each of us has a soul. If you asked the average believer to explain what the soul is, you would probably get a range of answers: the life-principle, life force, ego, mind, personality, the real self, the part of the person that lives on after death. While my body will one day die and decay, I should look to it that my soul is saved.

I suspect that the average Christian thinks of the soul as the real self, a self that is non-bodily, immaterial and therefore immortal. The body tends to be viewed more as a dwelling place of this soul-self, and a temporary one at that, for at death the soul is separated from the body and enters eternal reward or punishment. This may be an over-simplified view of things, but I believe that it does in fact lead many Christians to a rather dualistic view of the human person. As a matter of fact, the concepts of body and soul as they are commonly used owe more to ancient Greek philosophy (especially the various forms of

Platonism) and subsequent cultural and philosophical developments in the West (especially Descartes), rather than to the biblical understanding of the human person, which views the person
as an integral whole.

Scriptural Roots

Let us turn to the Scriptures to see what they may tell us about
the human person and its make-up. In English Bibles, "soul"
usually translates the OT Hebrew word *nepeš*, but it means something much broader: "breath," "life-blood," "life," or quite
simply "person" or "self." In Gen 2:7 we read that when God
blew the breath of life into Adam, Adam became a *nepeš*, a "living being."Hebrew does not have a special word for body. In the
Psalms, however, we find many examples of parallelism, in which
the word for flesh (*bāśār*) or other body words like heart (*lēb*),
are used as *synonyms* of soul and not to designate a contrasting
(or opposing!) component part. For example, "O God, you are
my God whom I seek; for you my flesh pines and my soul thirsts
. . ." (Ps 63:2). Soul and flesh, either alone or together, stand
for the total living person.

Both human beings and the other animals are animated by *rûaḥ*
or *nišmâ*, both of which mean "breath" or "life force" (Gen 2:7;
7:22). It is sometimes even identified with the very *rûaḥ* of God
(Job 33:4; 34:14). But it does not refer to the "real self" or individual person as something distinct from the body.

It is striking that the Hebrews associated what we think of as
"spiritual" activities with parts of the body. The heart is the organ
of intelligence, will and desire; the liver and kidneys are the organs
of conscience, grief or bitterness. Thinking, feeling and willing
are conceived holistically as interrelated, bodily activities. Reduc-
tion of life or self to a soul, or to the body for that matter, is
unknown.

Turning to the NT, we find soul (*psychē*) and flesh (*sarx*) used
in much the same way. *Psychē* refers to real, physical, individual,
flesh and blood, mortal life. "The Son of Man has come . . .
to give his *psychē* in ransom for the many" (Mk 10:45). In Acts
2:43 *pasa psychē* means "everybody" (no pun intended). It includes the whole realm of feelings, emotions and attitudes (Mk

14:34; Lk 2:35). Like its OT counterpart *bāśār, sarx* almost always means the whole, living human being or humanity as a whole. Paul uses it to highlight the creaturely, vulnerable and mortal nature of life (1 Cor 1:29, 15:39; Rom 6:19; Phil 3:3) especially as it stands under the judgment of God (Rom 3:20; Gal 2:16). Flesh is not a material part of the human person to be contrasted with an immaterial part. Nor is the flesh simply a bodiliness we share in common with other animals in distinction to the soul we alone possess (1 Cor 15:39). Rather, it is a way of referring specifically to human reality and to the whole of it, particularly as it has become infected by sin and death, and therefore in opposition to God (Gal 5:13; Rom 7:18).

This is precisely the point of Paul's central contrast between flesh and spirit (*pneuma*). The issue is not the opposition between body and soul, but the opposition between a sinful humanity and the Spirit of the holy God. Writing of the resurrection to the Corinthians, he says: "A natural body (*sōma psychikon*, "soulish body!") is sown and a spiritual body (*sōma pneumatikon*) comes up" (1 Cor 15:44). Earlier in the same letter, Paul distinguishes between one who has been given the spirit (*pneumatikos*) and one who is still soul (*psychikos*) or flesh (*sarkikos*) "of this world" (1 Cor 2:13-3:3).

For Paul, body (*sōma*) refers neither to a corpse nor to the complement of a soul (*psychē*) as the true self or ego. As Corinthians 15 shows, the resurrection of the body is understood to be God's creative transformation of mortal bodiliness as such (compare Rom 8:11). It is God's action upon the total person, not simply the on-going survival of some "immortal" part of the self.

Perhaps we should pay more serious attention to Paul when he says, "For this perishable nature must put on the imperishable, and this mortal nature must put on immortality" (1 Cor 15:53). The point is precisely the fact that it is the whole of our lived, corruptible, mortal human lives which will really enter into the life of the resurrection. Death is really swallowed up (v. 54) by the Spirit of God, not simply avoided by an immortal soul! This is really what makes the Christian doctrine about the resurrection of the body so startling (and to some in Corinth, ludicrous) compared to Plato's teaching about an immortal soul. Of course, Paul is not talking about the resuscitation of corpses but a transformation so wondrous in nature that he does not try to describe it.

The Gospel of salvation is the promise of the resurrection of the body, not escape from it. Seen in its cosmic fullness, God has come to save the world, not to save us from it. There may be truth in the familiar saying "You can't take it with you" but it is our faith that *God will* take us and everything of our world and transform it into a new heaven and a new earth.

With this we have reached the heart of the matter. While both the OT and the NT speak of body and soul, we have seen that both these terms refer to the human being in its concrete totality. Body and soul are not composite parts, but different ways of describing the complex living reality of the single, total human person. The challenge of the Gospel is not "Save your soul!" but "Open your entire living self (divided not by body/soul but by sin) to the living, life-giving Spirit of God!". If we do this, the Gospel assures us, we *have* eternal life.

Church Doctrine and Theology

The biblical view of human persons seems quite different from some of the philosophical views which have become influential in Western thought, notably those which center upon a body/soul contrast. The Bible is not very interested in such a distinction or contrast. We shall consider the one significant exception in the NT, the fate of the dead before the general resurrection, in a later chapter. What about official church teaching concerning the body and the soul? How can one understand it correctly against the background both of philosophical and Biblical thought?

The fact that church doctrine quickly adopted a non-biblical terminology to explain its biblically rooted faith is neither surprising nor inauthentic. It attempts to respond to specific questions which are posed in a certain context and within a particular linguistic and philosophical framework. Doctrine must be more than simple repetition of the Bible if it is to be effective. It makes use of various images and philosophical concepts to state and explain its biblical faith but it does not present these themselves for belief. This means that the language and concepts are not written in stone. We must attend to the biblical truth which doctrine attempts to express.

Using the terminology of body and soul, the church has consistently rejected those views which *reduce* the human person to something essentially material (one could ask if we really know what that means) or spiritual (the constant tendency in Christianity). Some forms of dualistic, spiritualizing thought went so far as to claim that the body and the material world were inherently evil and the work of an evil demi-god (Gnosticism and Manichaeism). Such views were rejected very early by theologians like Irenaeus and councils at Braga in 561 and Lateran IV in 1215. In the thirteenth century, Thomas Aquinas devised a brilliant synthesis of Christian faith with newly rediscovered Aristotelian philosophy and proposed what would become a classic formulation for theology: the soul is the substantial form of the body. He emphasized a *real distinction* of dimensions in a unity *without separation*. The body and soul are not two separate entities which are joined together. There can be no body without a soul as its inner form of existence and expression. Similarly, there can be no such thing as a human soul which is not related to the body. (This is why the church has rejected theories about the pre-existence of souls and taught that the soul is created directly by God as a person comes into existence.) I do not simply *have* a body and a soul. I *am* a body; I *am* a soul. In more current terms: I am bodily spirit or spiritual body.

We find this echoed in official church doctrine, which (often unlike its pastoral practice) emphasized the fundamental unity and goodness of the human person, calling the "rational and intellectual soul" the "form of the human body" (Vienne 1312). But Thomas and the council notwithstanding, dualistic Platonism, already so influential in Patristic theology, has had a far more significant and lasting effect.

The documents of Vatican II generally avoid body/soul terminology, both when considering the human condition and when speaking of salvation. *Gaudium et Spes* speaks of the "spiritual and immortal soul" but only after first stressing the essential unity of the human person and the goodness and dignity of the human body. God calls human persons in their "entire being" to an endless sharing of divine life (GS 18). While stating that the human person is "superior to bodily concerns," it avoids saying that the soul is superior to the body, content to affirm that in recognizing a spiritual and immortal soul, we are getting to the "depths of the very truth of the matter" (GS 14).

May we not say quite literally that spirit *is* the depth and truth of matter? With Rahner we may call the body the real symbol of the spirit. This does not mean that the body is "only" a symbol for the real self, but that the body is the reality in and through which the spirit is really present and without which it is not truly human spirit. These two dimensions are found inseparably in the mystery of the single human person in a way that is not clearly distinguishable: I, a self who exists only as body but refuses to be reduced simply to body. Language and ordinary experience bear this out. We say "I *am* (some)body" and "I *have* a body." My body is "me" but it is "my" body. Who says "my" to the body?

Unity and Totality

Theologians like Rahner and Teilhard de Chardin have stressed not only the basic unity of human persons in irreducibly different dimensions of body and spirit but also the fundamental unity of matter and spirit in the world. Spirit is the capacity for embodiment; matter longs to come to self-consciousness and expression as spirit and freedom. The Christian doctrine of creation holds that the created, finite world in the totality of those aspects, which may be called material and spiritual, ("visible and invisible" as the Creed says), has its unity and goodness in the unity and goodness of God who is its origin and final fulfillment. It is the whole world, and in particular, the whole human person, not just a soul, who is created in God's image, loved and destined to be one with God. The good news about the Kingdom is addressed to human beings in the totality of their lives.

Why is it worthwhile to emphasize the unity of the human being and its calling to divine life, rather than stressing the primacy of the soul and its immortal nature? History shows that the body/soul framework, if not in theory, certainly in practice, has often led to a denigration of the body (particularly sexuality), to a notion of grace which lost any contact with experience, to an attitude of disdain or neglect of "worldly things," to a view of salvation which meant escape from the body and the world, and to a notion of the Kingdom which had little to do with this world and our responsibility for it. It is supremely paradoxical that body/soul language, which was developed as a way of combatting dualistic and reductionistic views of the human person, has in fact tended to promote such views into our own day.

If, encouraged by the Bible, we try to understand human persons in the world in a more holistic way, we may avoid some of these mistakes and exaggerations and understand the Gospel promise and challenge more deeply. Striving for a way of life which integrates these two dimensions is not just a trendy question of health and well-being. It is a question of final wholeness, of salvation. Thus, the message of the Gospel about the goodness of the earth, the dignity of human life and the demands of God's justice and love, orients Christians to the needs of the whole person and of the whole earth.

We are challenged to turn away from sin, not from the body or from the world. The enemy of the spirit is not the body; the enemy of the spirit/body is sin. We must take care not to make cults of either body or soul. Today, it is more often than not the soul, sickened by fear, despair or addiction, which drags the body down, not the other way around! And not only our own bodies, but the body of our mother earth. The church, which has often fostered a one-sided preoccupation with the soul, faces a great challenge and must undergo continued conversion if it is going to be able to respond credibly to the equally exaggerated cult of body, youth and health which characterizes American society today.

In the process, let us not forget what, at its best, the traditional language of body and soul tried to express and remind us of: the divine depth and destiny of the ordinary, and the unique capacity and responsibility we have as transcendent beings to enter into free and active relationship with others, with the world and with God, and so to shape in some way the future to which God calls all of creation.

RELATED READING

Karl Rahner, "The Body in the Order of Salvation" in *Theological Investigations 17* (New York: Crossroad, 1981), 71–89 and "The Unity of Spirit and Matter in the Christian Understanding" in *Theological Investigations 6* (New York: Seabury Press, 1974), 153–77 address the problem of dualism and the tendency toward spiritualization in Christianity. Peter Brown, *The Body and Society: Men, Women and Sexual Renunciation in Early Christianity* (New York: Columbia University Press, 1988) is an extraordinary study of early Christian attitudes toward the body.

6

Sin

Christianity's teaching about sin has been called the most easily verified of its doctrines. This may be an exaggeration but we are all well aware of the evil which marks our lives and for which we are responsible. The church teaches that the voice of conscience within every person summons us to obey a fundamental moral law inscribed in our hearts by God: "Love the good and avoid evil." In particular instances it may speak more specifically: do this, do not do that (GS 16). There is right and wrong; there are Dos and Don'ts. For most people, therefore, to sin is to do something wrong, to go against one's conscience, to disobey the Ten Commandments or some other rule governing church life. Most catholics were taught that some sins are relatively minor ("venial"), others so serious that they are called deadly ("mortal"). The rationale behind the classification was not always clear. It used to be a mortal sin to eat meat on Friday; now it's not a sin at all. On the other hand, today the church speaks much more clearly than before about social sin, emphasizing that sin is not just a question of isolated individual acts, but a reality that has a social and structural dimension. What makes something a sin? What is really the essence of sin?

Biblical Perspectives

The biblical account of sin begins in Genesis 3 with the Yahwist's story of the "fall" of Adam and Eve. Its purpose is to explain why the world is filled with so much suffering, alienation and, finally, death. In what might be called the first theodicy (a term coined much later by the 17/18th century Jewish philosopher Leibnitz, referring to a justification of God in the face of the evil and suffering we experience in God's world), the answer is given that human beings, not God or some other demi-god, are responsible. The image of the garden of Eden, like the later Priestly narrative which precedes it in Genesis 1, tells us that the world as created and desired by God was good, full of life and harmony. Adam and Eve were given every good thing and virtually unrestricted freedom. From the tree in the middle of the garden alone they were not to eat; otherwise they would die. Still, tempted by the serpent, they managed to disobey the single commandment given them by God and were sorely punished for this transgression. From the pangs of birth to the final hour of death, every manner of suffering and evil in life has resulted from this "original" sin, either as God's punishment or as its inevitable effect. The sexes became estranged from each other, both alienated from the environment. They must sweat and toil to stay alive. Before they die, the "first parents" see their first child murdered by his own brother. In succeeding chapters (4-11) we learn that human evil spread so quickly that God repented of having created humans and destroyed them by a flood, saving the animals and one small family. The ancient writers apparently understood even the lack of communication in the "Babel" of different languages and cultures as a result and symbol of the destruction of the community between humanity and God. The rest, as they say, is history, and a pretty grim one at that.

Sin is seen as a transgression of a divine command, rebellion against God and God's authority. But all of this for breaking one rule? It would be a great mistake to view this in such an abstract and legalistic way, since God's sovereignty is never a question of mere power or arbitrary authority. What is really at issue in the story is something deeper. The serpent claims that, far from killing them, the tree's fruit will make them like God. Adam and Eve begin to believe that God was lying to them, holding something back from them, something desirable and perhaps even necessary. Suddenly they are not satisfied with the way God made them. Reading this story together with the Priestly account as it appears in the Bible, one sees a certain irony. Created in the image and likeness of God and found to be good in God's eyes, the first humans, in their own eyes, were neither. In eating the fruit which seems to promise them what they want, the human beings decide to be their own gods, since God's designs for them were evidently not loving or trustworthy. Seen in this way, their disobedience is not so much the mere transgression of a command as it is a turning away from God in the heart.

If we look throughout the OT, we find a number of different words for sin, each of which points to a particular dimension of the reality of sin. *Ḥaṭṭā* means "missing the mark" or "misdeed." *'Āwôn* means "guilt" or "iniquity" and refers to twisted interior state of the sinner. *Peša'* means "rebellion," "hostility" or "obstinacy" before God. This last word is the one frequently used in Exodus and throughout the prophetic writings to express the infidelity (Hosea, Jeremiah), pride (Amos, Isaiah) or ingratitude (Isaiah, Jeremiah) of the people as a whole in abandoning the Covenant, the central expression of God's graciousness and fidelity as Creator, Savior and Sustainer.

More than any other passage, I think Moses' farewell speech in Deut 30:15-20 brings out the real nature and tragedy of sin. "See, I have set before you this day life and good, death and evil. If you obey the commandments of the Lord your God which I command you this day, by loving the Lord your God, by walking in God's ways, and by keeping God's commandments, statutes and ordinances, then you shall live and multiply, and the Lord your God will bless you in the land which you are entering to take possession of it. But if your heart turns away, and you will not hear, but are drawn away to worship other gods and serve them, I declare you this day that you shall perish; you shall not live long in the land which you are going over the Jordan to enter and possess . . . therefore choose life, that you and your descendants may live, loving the Lord your God, obeying God's voice, and cleaving to God; for that means life to you and length of days . . ."

In all its forms, sin consists in turning away from God with a hardened heart and stiffened neck (Ps 95:8; Jer 7:24-26). It means saying No to the only one who is capable of offering life that will last. At its root, sin is idolatry. As the prophets did not tire of warning, no life can come from gods who are made of stone and wood by mortal hands. Since the Lord alone is God, who created the heavens and the earth, such a turning from God is suicidal; it can only lead to death.

It is important to see the connection between the sovereignty of God and the Covenant life of the people. No doubt a direct and explicitly idolatrous denial of God leads to sins of injustice and disintegration of the community. But the reverse is just as true and more often the case. Selfishness, greed, revenge and all those other forms of injustice that destroy the life of the community are the ordinary, everyday forms of idolatry (Am 5:21-25; Mi 6:6-8). In turning our hearts away from our brothers and sisters, we turn away from God.

Only God can forgive sin. Just as Covenant and communion are God's free gift, so forgiveness and restoration to communion are also a free gift. Sin-offerings and sacrifices of reparation are of no avail unless there is real conversion of heart. A humble spirit and a contrite heart will not be despised by God (Ps 51:17). Those who forsake their evil ways and seek the Lord can expect abundant pardon (Is 55:7). "Bless the Lord, O my soul, and forget not all God's benefits, who forgives all your iniquity, who heals all your diseases, who redeems your life from the Pit, who crowns you with steadfast love and mercy . . ." (Ps 103:2-4).

All of this forms the background of the NT, where we find a similarity of usage. *Paraptōma* means "misstep." *Parabasis* means "transgression" and usually refers to sin as a violation of the Law. *Hamartia* means "missing the mark," especially in the plural, when it refers to a variety of sinful actions. As in the OT, sin is a personal, deliberate action. It is a communal reality, to be sure, but no one can hide and shift the blame, whether to one's ancestors, parents, peers or "situation." Sin is something which springs from the heart of the person and for which every individual is ultimately responsible.

There is more to the reality of sin, however, than individual sinful acts. It is state or condition of *anomia*, "lawlessness" or *adikia*, "injustice." It is a hardening of the heart (Heb 3:13) and a willful blindness (Jn 9:40f), something which characterizes the very interior of the sinner who willfully turns away from God. This is especially evident in the use of *hamartia* in the singular. According to Paul, who speaks about sin more than any other

NT writer, it is a power which has sway over all humankind, a power to which we are slaves and from which we must be redeemed. It is clearly more than merely the sum of sinful deeds. In describing his own experience, Paul says that it is a force at work within, which enslaves his true self (Rom 7:17-20). It rules as a law, causes war in the inner self (7:22f) and leads ultimately to death (7:24; 8:2).

The specific reality of sin in the NT must be seen in relationship to the person and mission of Jesus Christ, in whom God is personally present to bestow forgiveness and life upon sinners. In his preaching, Jesus shifts the emphasis away from ritual observance and restores the "Great Commandments" to their proper centrality. Sin and repentance are seen in terms of the Gospel of the Kingdom and the demands of God's merciful justice. For John, sin is the refusal to believe in the Son whom the Father has sent (Jn 16:9). Finally, it is a question of love (Gal 5:14). In the moving story which Jesus told about a father and his two sons (Lk 15:11-32), sin is seen as a refusal to accept and live according to God's free gift of love. And, as Matthew 25 makes clear, the Lord of Love meets us most of all in the faces of the poor, the sick and the forgotten.

The Social Dimension of Sin

While sin is the free, personal act of an individual, both the OT and the NT emphasize the fact that sin is a social reality. In his *Apostolic Exhortation on Reconciliation and Penance* (1984), John Paul II develops what Vatican II only touched upon. Every sin, he states, even the "most intimate and secret one, the most strictly individual one" has repercussions on the whole community and in some measure upon the whole human family (16). Whatever he may have in mind, it seems that most sin, in fact, is a *direct* offense or failure of love toward the neighbor. While we are accustomed to thinking of injustice and hardheartedness against individuals as sinful, the Pope reminds us that we "sin against the common good and its exigencies in relation to the whole broad spectrum of the rights and duties of citizens" in political, social and economic matters, a point forcefully made by the American bishops in their recent pastoral letter on the econ-

omy. On a larger scale, class struggle, obstinate confrontation between blocs of nations, racial or ethnic oppression are all examples
of the profound evil which infects social structures as a result of
personal sin. Only a renewed sense of the reality of such sin, precisely as an affront to God, and the conversion of the sinner can
bring about lasting peace and justice.

The Inescapability of Sin

In Romans 5, Paul graphically describes the radical, universal
and mortal power of sin. Hearkening back to the Yahwist tradition of Genesis 2-11, he states that "sin came into the world
through one human being and death through sin, and so death
spread to all men and women because all sinned" (5:12). Death
is the reality and power of sin become visible. No one can escape
its power (compare 1 Cor 15:21f).

This famous passage formed the scriptural basis for the doctrine of original sin. According to this teaching, all human beings are born into a world which has been deeply wounded from
the very beginning by human sin. None of us, therefore, can escape the effects of sin, even those sins for which we are not personally responsible. This does not mean that God punishes us for
the sins of others. (And it certainly does not mean that unbap-
tized infants are excluded from heaven!) It simply means that as
individual human beings, we can never escape the "human condition" of the whole. Our freedom is not free. We are not capable on our own of loving the world and God as we ought. God
alone can break the power of sin and reconcile us to God's self
and this is precisely what God has done in Jesus Christ.

As Karl Rahner and Piet Schoonenberg point out, to say that
all men and women are guilty of or born with original sin is very
misleading. First of all, "sin" really means those personal actions
which I myself perform and for which I am therefore responsible.
I am certainly affected by the real sins of others, but I am not
personally accountable for them. Second, this doctrine is not simply concerned with an "original" personal sinful act of the first
human beings, the first in a string of subsequent sins. It is concerned with the fact that it is a lasting *basis* of the sinful condition of the human world in its real history. It is not only "original"

but "originating." Perhaps it would be a good idea to abandon the term "original sin" and speak, rather, of the universality and inescapability of sin which threatens the world and every person in it. In any case, while the ability of each to love the good and to avoid evil has clearly been affected by others, the doctrine of "original sin" also demands that we recognize the real and lasting effects of our sins on others.

The Universality of God's Grace

For Paul, the universality of sin, the solidarity of all human beings as sinners and sin's deadly power are obvious from human experience. He was not interested in developing a doctrine of original sin. That would have been to belabor the obvious. To understand what it really means to be human, Paul's focus is not on origins (protology) but on final destiny (eschatology). In Christ, the final "end" of humanity is revealed. Paul sought, therefore, to explain the finality and universality of God's gracious, saving action in Jesus Christ. How could the life, death and resurrection of a single human being, Jesus Christ, be of final, saving significance for all men and women?

"Adam" is the first-born of the human race which suffers enslavement and death because of sin. As such, he is a figure of Christ (5:14), the "final Adam," who by obedience became the first-born from the dead, the one who destroys death and gives life (1 Cor 15:45). But the gift of God in Christ far surpasses the offense of Adam (Rom 5:15-17) and brings righteousness and life for all (5:18f). The real subject of Romans 5, and of any correct doctrine of original sin based on it, is the good news about the saving action of God in Christ which "originates" grace for us all while "we were yet sinners" (5:8). Christian life, therefore, exists in a dialectic of sin and grace. While we are all children of "Adam" as sinners, we have been made children of God in grace. This grace, God's love and life-giving power, is nothing less than participation in the divine life of the Spirit. It was God's plan even *before* the "beginning" of the world (Eph 1:3-10). This leads us directly to the next chapter.

RELATED READING

Piet Schoonenberg, *Man and Sin* (Notre Dame: The University of Notre Dame Press, 1965) is still one of the finest books on the subject. Karl Rahner, "The Sin of Adam" in *Theological Investigations 11* (New York: Seabury, 1974), 247-62; "Guilt—Responsibility—Punishment within the View of Catholic Theology" and "Justified and Sinner at the Same Time" in *Theological Investigations 6* (New York: Seabury, 1974), 197-217, 218-30 are his most important articles in this area. Bernard Häring, *Free and Faithful in Christ: Moral Theology for Clergy and Laity 1: General Moral Theology* (New York: Seabury Press, 1978) has a good chapter on sin and conversion. M. Scott Peck, *People of the Lie* (New York: Simon and Schuster, 1983) offers penetrating psychological reflections.

7

Grace: The Gift of God's Life

"Grace to you and peace from God our Father and the Lord Jesus Christ." Following the custom of his time, Paul began his letters with a short prayer of blessing upon the recipients. But for Paul, these words are much more than "Christianized" etiquette. They express in concise form his whole understanding of the Christ event as saving grace. How are we Christians today to understand what grace is?

Biblical Background

Turning to the Scriptures, we find many references to grace in both the OT and the NT. In the OT, we find the closely related words *ḥēn* and *ḥesed*. *Ḥēn* expresses the gracious approach of a person to someone who is weaker, poorer and in need of help. It refers both to the graciousness of the benefactor and to the favor or gift bestowed. It is used to express God's Covenant graciousness and mercy, which is the basis of confident prayer for healing (Ps 6:2), rescue and redemption (Ps 26:11) and pardon for sin (Ps 51:1f).

Ḥesed is often rendered as "loving-kindness" or "goodness." It is more than an act of help or mercy. It implies an on-going relationship of concern, even friendship. In the OT, this word takes on enormous significance as a description of God's attitude toward Israel. Above all, God's loving-kindness and fidelity is seen in the Covenant, which is the expression of God's gracious turning to Israel in need (Ex 20:6). In a liturgical setting, the

Psalms recount the mighty deeds of love and mercy which are the substance of God's *ḥesed* and proclaim it as the sure foundation for Israel's life and future. It is a source of forgiveness (25:7) and deliverance (44:26). Prophets like Hosea, Jeremiah and Isaiah called upon the people to let the Lord's gracious love inform the life of the community. God's grace is the norm for the community's justice.

In the Septuagint, *charis* is the translation of *ḥēn,* and closely associated with *ḥesed*. It means "attractiveness" or "favor" from God, God's good gifts. The element of gratuity is stressed and developed in Philo and later rabbinical writings. The grace which constitutes the perfection or complete goodness of human beings is something which is God's achievement, not something which human beings can secure themselves.

In the NT, *charis*, although occurring only rarely in the Gospels, becomes a central term for Paul. Usually rendered by the word "grace," it is the fundamental concept for expressing his understanding of the salvation event. It stands for the totality of salvation freely bestowed by God in Christ (Tit 2:11). As in secular Greek and Hellenistic Judaism, *charis* highlights the gracious condescension of the giver and the thanks of the one favored. It is the *gratuity* of God's saving action which is central for Paul. Grace is unearned. It is not based on worthiness (Rom 3:24), human merit (Rom 4:4), or religious observance (Rom 3:27f), but on God's fidelity (1 Cor 1:4-9) and faith (Rom 4:16).

Closely connected with the gratuity of grace is its *universality*. Something is not a gift because only some receive it, even though I suspect that is the way we usually think. God's gift never excludes. Grace is freely given and given freely to *all* men and women (Tit 2:11). All men and women are justified through it (Rom 3:24; 5:12-17).

Charis is the surprising, unearned breaking-in of God who saves. It is not opposed to the world but to the power of sin, which has come to enslave the world. It is more than just a favor or benefit. It overcomes sin (Rom 5:20) and becomes the new reigning power of God in the world (Rom 6:14; 8:2). While death is the power of sin, grace is the power for life (Rom 5:21). It makes generosity possible (2 Cor 8:1) and its goal is every good work (2 Cor 9:8). Love is the heart of grace, both the divine favor for

God's people and for the relationships which should obtain in the community, the body of Christ. God's relationship with the people enables and demands the same kind of compassion, mercy and gracious turning to others.

This is why grace is so closely associated with the Holy Spirit (Tit 3:7), which is poured into the hearts of believers and makes them one in Christ. Grace is the presence of the Spirit of Christ, a new way of being, a milieu "in which we stand," the life of the Spirit poured into our hearts (Rom 5:2-5). It is bestowed in concrete ways as a gift or charism (*charisma*) according to the freedom of the Spirit of Christ who, in different ways, according to the "analogy of faith," thereby builds up the body of Christ (Rom 12:3-8; 1 Cor 12).

It is not an invisible, metaphysical reality beyond our everyday experience. It is seen and experienced in the body of Christ, the community of believers. Here, above all, is where grace longs to become visible. For Paul, it is seen in the love, forgiveness and service of community life. Grace and mission go hand in hand. For Paul, grace brings freedom (from the power of sin and death). But freedom, as *the* basic grace or gift of the Spirit, is an opportunity for service (Galatians 5). That is how we participate in Christ's mission of service. Thus the grace of salvation as new life in the Spirit is intimately connected with the particular "gifts" of the Spirit and becomes visible even now as ministry and service in the life of the community and its mission as church.

Historical Developments

The church developed its teaching on grace over a long period of time. It began in the controversies surrounding Pelagius and Augustine in the early fifth century. Pelagius reasoned that if human beings were morally responsible before God for their actions, they must be able, even without the help of God, to do the good and attain salvation. Augustine, marvelling that good is possible at all in the world as we experience it, insisted that God's grace was necessarily at work. Without it, human freedom is so wounded, so unfree, that it could never do anything good. God's grace, therefore, is a force that frees human freedom from its bondage to self and sin and establishes true human autonomy *with* the Spirit of God working within, not apart from it. In the course of these debates, Augustine formulated his teaching about the universality of sin ("original sin") and the necessity of grace, which was to have a significant effect on theology and church life. Much of his teaching received official status at the Synod of Orange (529). Despite this, the influence of Pelagius and later forms of his ideas ("semi-Pelagianism") continued to grow, often leading to a kind of rigid asceticism and spiritual elitism: salvation can and must be earned by moral perfection.

In the thirteenth century, Thomas Aquinas tried to reconcile God's justice and human freedom with the gratuity and necessity of grace. He contended that the life of grace, as a participation in God's very being, was "supernatural," exceeding and completing (though not destroying or supplanting) "nature." Thus, whereas Augustine had viewed grace primarily in a moral context, Thomas reflected on grace in ontological terms. For him, grace was not essential and gratuitous merely because of human sin, but because human "nature" of itself is incapable of the divine end to which it is ordained. Grace elevates human beings and infuses them with a new "nature" proportionate to their divine, "supernatural" destiny. With the help of supernatural grace we are enabled to do what by nature we are unable to do.

Unfortunately, as the situation of the church at the time of the Reformation clearly shows, this "help" was often understood in rather crass, reified terms. Grace often seemed to be something one could earn, either through good works or through various religious practices. Could one buy one's way into heaven? It seemed so in view of the widespread abuse of indulgences, a situation which contradicted the heart of the Gospel about the gratuity of God's grace.

These were some of the concerns of the Reformers, and of Martin Luther in particular. But for them, there was an important existential issue at stake. On what basis may the believer have confidence and certainty about his or her salvation? For them, certainly not on the basis of an "elevated nature" (much less because of "graces" accumulated through sacramental ritualism or indulgences). The Reformers stressed that only trust in God's forgiveness and promise ("faith alone," "grace alone") could assure the sinner of salvation. In baptism, the sinner, who has lost all likeness to God through sin, is declared by God to be justified even though he or she is and remains a sinner ("sinner and justified at the same time").

For its part, the catholic church, especially at the Council of Trent (1545-63), insisted that human beings were not totally perverted by sin and that by virtue of God's grace, effectively offered to believers in the sacraments, they are "totally justified" before God. Moreover, even though they may continue to sin, they are empowered and called upon to cooperate with grace in salutary works of love ("faith and works," "faith in action").

Today, we realize that in the heated polemics of the times, the two sides often argued against caricatures of each other's positions. Through the research of theologians like Hans Küng and Karl Rahner and the work of various ecumenical commissions, it seems that there are no longer church dividing differences of opinions here. We may affirm that God's grace is utterly free, wholly unearned, truly saving and manifest in loving action.

Implications for Today

In light of all this, a few observations may help to get to the heart of a Christian understanding of grace. First, grace is not a thing. It is more than a divine impulse, blessing or help at work in human beings ("created grace," "actual grace"). More than any other theologian, Karl Rahner has stressed that grace is first and foremost God's own divine life ("uncreated grace"). Giver and gift are one.[1] As divine love itself, God has only one "thing" to bless us with: God's own divine love and life. Grace, therefore, refers to God's own life as God shares it with us through Jesus Christ in the Holy Spirit. Instead of concentrating upon "graces" as different degrees of blessing or merit bestowed by God (as was often the case), we should focus upon *grace* (in the singular) as our life, lived in the Spirit.

Second, grace is not something foreign or opposed to creation. Traditionally, one has spoken of "supernatural" grace. But it must be emphasized that grace is not something simply above or separate, certainly not opposed, to "nature," although such ter-

[1]Karl Rahner, *Foundations of Christian Faith* (New York: Seabury, 1978) 120.

minology often seemed to imply just that. Grace is the final perfection and fulfillment of "nature." Even more radically,
however, "nature" is itself the expression of grace, since, as I
have already suggested, creation is the result of God's desire to
bestow divine love. As Rahner once wrote, "Nature is because
grace had to be."[2] Even though they are distinct, therefore, they
must be seen together, as one. Grace is the deepest center of nature. To speak of grace as "supernatural" may be one way of
highlighting the fact that the world finds its own truest fulfillment, not in itself, but in God. But we are not called to another,
different, "supernatural world." God calls *us and this world* (we
could not be human without our world) to its true fulfillment in
a relationship of loving union with God. Our very "nature" or
essence as human creatures, says Rahner, is constituted by such
an orientation ("supernatural existential").[3]

Third, grace, which is revealed in its final and definitive fullness through Jesus Christ in the Holy Spirit, has been the goal
and driving force of God's creative action from "before the foundation of the world" (Eph 1:4). The grace of Christ did not enter
the world for the first time 2,000 years ago. It has been a constitutive principle of creation from the start. God's saving self-offer
in grace, therefore, has always and everywhere been present and
effective in some way.

Vatican II clearly states that God's saving Spirit is not limited
to or controlled by the visible church. Grace is at work in the
hearts of all who sincerely follow the dictates of their conscience,
even if they are not explicit believers (LG 15-16; GS 22). In
celebrating the Sacraments and proclaiming the Good News of
salvation in Christ, therefore, the church does not bring grace into
an otherwise graceless world. Its worship is important, Rahner
reminds us, not because something happens in it that does not
happen anywhere else, but because there, the church gratefully
proclaims in Christ the divine depth of ordinary life, life which
has always been enfolded and blessed by grace.[4] The church will

---

[2]Karl Rahner, "On the Theology of Worship," *Theological Investigations 19* (New York: Crossroad, 1983) 143.

[3]For a concise treatment of this idea see *Foundations of Christian Faith*, 126-33.

[4]"On the Theology of Worship," 147.

understand itself more and more as a grace-empowered witness to the real presence and challenge of grace in the world, rather than as the sole possessor or dispenser of that grace.

Fourth, grace is opposed to sin, not to nature. Sin is a permanent and pervasive reality from which the world as a whole and each one of us personally suffer. From the very start it has compromised human freedom and the final good of universal loving communion in God toward which it is directed. Human freedom must itself be freed. Thus God's grace is present not only as the gift of freedom but as the on-going call of conversion to truer, deeper freedom.

Finally, the life of grace is not a life different from our "real" everyday lives. This is where the gift and the challenge of grace is given, where the conflict between sin and grace is real. This is why, in the spirit of Matthew 25, traditional piety correctly spoke about the corporal and spiritual works of *mercy* and why the American bishops have repeatedly emphasized the intrinsic connection between faith and *justice*. As the parable of the merciless official (Mt 18:21-35) shows, God's grace is to be the norm for our justice.

Where do we *experience* grace, the divine life shared with us through Christ, the healing, transforming and saving Spirit of God? Certainly the Scriptures and the Sacraments have played an important role in the lives of believers. Paul speaks of the freedom, reconciliation and loving service which are the heart of community life. The signs and fruits of grace are not always (or usually!) extraordinary mystical events. Often they are not even explicitly religious.

Grace is experienced in those "limit situations" when, faced with Mystery which evades all our attempts to understand life's paradoxes and contradictions, we embrace it gratefully in its joys and sorrows, hopes and despairs. We experience grace in those surprising, unexpected moments when we feel ourselves in the presence of an incomprehensible, extraordinary depth: the birth of a child, the power of the sea, the beauty of a great work of art.

There is indeed something like a "mysticism of ordinary life," as Rahner called it.[5] For it is also grace when "falling in love"

---

[5]*Ibid.*, 148.

stands the test of "remaining in love," when women and men find the strength and generosity required of parents, when those who are oppressed find the courage and confidence to assert themselves in dignity, when sickness and suffering are borne with patience and hope, when enemies forgive one another and nations lay down their weapons.

Recognized or not, grace is present and active wherever human beings accept themselves for what they are before God and realize their true humanity. Grace is experienced whenever men and women are reconciled in love with one another and with God. For grace leads the human person to that fullness of life which is only found outside its own narrow, enclosed "self." Grace, as the fullness of our lives created and blessed by God, means the holiness and wholeness of all together (Eph 1:7-10).

RELATED READING

Karl Rahner has influenced me more than any other contemporary theologian, and this chapter shows how true that is with respect to a theology of grace. "On the Theology of Worship" in *Theological Investigations 19* (New York: Crossroad, 1983), 141-49 is an especially beautiful and concise presentation of Rahner's understanding of nature and grace. "Nature and Grace" in *Theological Investigations 4* (Baltimore: Helicon Press, 1966), 165-88 is his key essay on the subject. "Experience of the Holy Spirit" in *Theological Investigations 18* (New York: Crossroad, 1983), 189-210 is a very fine meditation on the experience of grace. Roger Haight, *The Experience and Language of Grace* (New York: Paulist Press, 1979) presents an historical and systematic survey and is the best book of its kind available. I have found it very useful in teaching and helpful in preparing these reflections. Anne E. Carr, *Transforming Grace* (San Francisco: Harper and Row, 1988) is especially valuable since it approaches the main themes surrounding grace and salvation from the perspective of women's experience.

8

The Mystery of Death

In the last chapter we spoke of grace as God's gracious self-bestowal in love through the life, death and resurrection of Christ. If we die to sin, the life we live even now "in the Spirit" will reach its final and lasting fullness in God when we are united with Christ in a resurrection like his (Rom 6:5; 8:9-11) and share in the divine life itself. At that time, Christ will appear in glory and destroy death, the final enemy (1 Cor 15:26). But until then, the life of grace remains in the shadow of death.

Death: A Fact of Life

Death is a fact of life, both inevitable and universal; there is no avoiding it. But death resists being treated *merely* as a fact of life. It is the fact which threatens life absolutely, not only at the final moment of death, but from the very beginning. It gives life its radical uncertainty, final seriousness and ultimate mystery.

Death threatens us on many levels. The precariousness of peace, the threat of nuclear war, world hunger and the AIDS epidemic have a profound impact. We quickly lose an adolescent sense of immortality when our loved ones die, when we are betrayed or when we suffer a debilitating disease. Political and economic oppression, sexism and prejudice can threaten and kill human life long before an EEG shows a flat zero line.

Death is what gives our lives a sense of urgency and ultimacy. If our lives were endless and endlessly revisable, then nothing would ever really have to get done, today, tomorrow, or ever!

Because we have a specific, limited time and space in which to accomplish something, we are forced to take our time and action seriously. What I do or do not do makes a difference. For most people, death is what makes us live with a profound sense of accountability. It makes each of us take stock of our lives and ask, "What have I done, what will I have done with my life?".

But here is precisely where the paradox of death for human beings becomes apparent. Though universally present as a "natural" part of the world as we experience it, and although it gives human life its unique sense of ultimacy, urgency and accountability, death is something which human beings have never been able to accept as "natural," even at the end of a long and full life. What is worse, of course, is that death often intrudes, tragically and ruthlessly, much earlier. We cannot accept death as something which ought to be. At some time, in some way, we all ask "Why must those whom I love die?". "Why must I die?"

Not being able to accept death as a proper part of life, most of us live in fear of it. We try to overcome it by denying it. We worship youth, health and beauty. We often avoid contact with the old, the sick and the dying, giving even the bodies of the dead rosy lips and cheeks. We don't like to look death in the face. I suspect that this is one reason why AIDS is so uniquely terrifying. It touches us everywhere, in a way we can no longer avoid, with the reality of death.

"Why must we die?" is a religious question, not a scientific one. Death is not merely a *biological* reality, but more fundamentally a personal, *existential* reality. Despite the attempts of science to prolong life, I do not imagine anyone would really like to live life as we know it indefinitely! "Why must we die?" is not only a question about death but also about our experience of life. Long before we are confronted with death, we wonder, "Is this all there is?". Neither life nor death ought to be as we experience them.

What does Christian faith have to say to our experience of death? Does it offer any answers to our questions? Can it invite us to a new way of experiencing both dying and living?

Sin and Death

According to the Scriptures, the world as we experience it is not as it ought to be, not as God intended it. As we have seen, the creation stories of Genesis both affirm the goodness of God in creating and the goodness of the world as God created it. What "ought to have been" is a world in which human beings lived in happiness and intimate harmony with God, one another and the world. According to the Yahwist tradition of Genesis 2-11, the grim realities of alienation, suffering and death are the consequences of human sin. This does not mean that God condemned the human race to death the way a judge imposes a sentence upon a convicted criminal. In the OT, suffering and death can be seen as the intrinsic and necessary consequence of sinful action itself, rather than as an additional penalty imposed by God. To turn away from the Lord is to die, not because the Lord strikes down the sinner, but because the sinner has abandoned the only source of real life there is (Dt 30:15-20). For that reason, God pleads with Israel through the prophets to repent of its idolatry, to turn back to the Lord and be saved. The Lord is God of the living not of the dead.

In Romans 5, Paul adopts this tradition in order to explain the universal power of the saving grace of Christ. Life as we know it, as we have chosen it, is ruled by sin and death. Through Adam's sin, death entered the world (5:12). It reigned through that one human being (5:17) bringing judgment and condemnation to all (5:16). Death cannot be seen, however, merely as a punishment suffered as the result of another's sins, for in fact all have sinned, so that death spread to all (5:12). Through God's free gift in Christ, however, grace abounds (5:15). It reigns through one human being's act of righteousness (5:17), bringing acquittal and life for all (5:18). Life "as it ought to be," as God has graciously willed it, is the life of grace we have received through Christ in the Holy Spirit.

Basing itself on Genesis 3 and Romans 5, church teaching about sin and grace, from the early Pelagian controversies, through the Reformation and down to the Second Vatican Council, appears to understand even biological death as the consequence of sin. In light of both scientific knowledge and modern biblical scholarship such a position would appear to be untenable. But even Paul, who probably *assumed* this to be true, is not really interested in biological death (or biological life, for that matter!). Ultimately, for Paul, life and death are more than mere biological realities. They are ways of talking about being in relationship with God or not. He is concerned with the *meaning and experience* of death, with the power it has to enslave us with fear and terror, and of life, as it finds freedom and fullness in the Spirit. Paul's perspective and purpose are evident in the opening lines of the chapter, where he assures believers that they may have peace with God, sure access to the grace in which they stand and reason, in every suffering, to rejoice in the hope of sharing the glory of God (5:1-5).

What gives death its sting is something quite independent of biological processes. It is sin (1 Cor 15:56). Apart from physical pain, perhaps what we fear and *humanly suffer* in death is radical loneliness, being completely isolated and cut off: not only from our loved ones but most especially from God. The emptiness, hopelessness and terror which mark death can be seen as manifestations of human sin which, long before the moment of death, have weakened and perhaps destroyed many of our life-giving relationships. The absence or remoteness of God is a real consequence of sin in our world and of our own personal sin in turning away from God. It is not a punishment inflicted by God, but the inescapable consequence of sin itself, not only of some "original" sin, but of our real personal sins.

Dying with Christ

As Karl Rahner has pointed out, biological death in itself need not be thought of merely as the tragic "end" and breakdown of life, but as a natural and desirable part of the created biological order in which real personal freedom has appeared.[1] For, as we have seen, the history of human freedom is not merely the opportunity to keep doing something different, but finally and

---

[1] Karl Rahner, "Ideas for a Theology of Death," *Theological Investigations 13* (New York: Seabury, 1975) 180.

definitively to accept God's gracious offer of love and so to share in divine life. Such a "fundamental option" takes shape in the actions of our everyday lives, but cannot achieve its definitive form except as the "end" of all possible changes. Thus death could be seen as a "finalization" of my life and all its specific choices. Coming to such an end would not only be desirable but absolutely necessary for human freedom, since by its very nature it is directed toward such final self-actualization before God.

But unless we have reason to hope that what has definitively taken shape in our lives will truly last, unless we have reason to hope for a final, forgiving and transforming completion of all that has remained partial or distorted, what ultimate reason could any human action have? What reason, then, is there to view death as a final consummation rather than ultimate nothingness?

Finally, the only "reason" or ground for hope that death is not only biological disintegration, but also the victorious integration of life in everlasting fullness, is the resurrection of Jesus. Such a life finds its glorious fulfillment in God and lasts forever. Jesus' resurrection was not a personal privilege or reward for Jesus but an act of God "for us and for our salvation." Jesus' resurrection is God's promise to us. What the Spirit accomplished in Jesus is the work of the Spirit in all of us. This is why Paul says that Jesus is the first born of many brothers and sisters (Rom 8:29) and why he insisted that Christian faith stands or falls with his resurrection (1 Cor 15:12-19). For believers it is good news about human destiny and an invitation in the power of the Spirit to imagine the hidden meaning of death darkened and obscured by sin.

From this it is clear that the Christian understanding and experience of death must be considered in light of the hope we have in Christ of resurrection. As *hope*, it is a free and trusting commitment in love to what seems and really is impossible for the person who hopes. What I truly hope for is something which I must finally receive from another. With hope in the *resurrection*, the believer looks beyond his or her own deeds to the incomprehensible God in the trust that the life he or she has lived will find *from* God and *in* God its ultimate end and completion. Ultimately then, to die with Christ in the hope of resurrection means to surrender one's life, with all its accomplishments and failures, dreams and disappointments, into the hands of God, who alone can raise it up into everlasting fullness.

Such surrender is really what life is always about. In addition to all the ways in which we learn to assert ourselves, control our own lives and the world around us and therefore establish our independence, we must also learn to surrender control over a great many things, to depend on others, to defer at times to their desires and needs and to establish personal relationships of mutual love and trust. Only in such relationships are we truly human. I can only grow as a person to the extent that I learn to surrender myself in trusting love to the mystery of others.

Only if we open our hearts to the divine Other, the Spirit of Christ, will we find the freedom and courage to love and serve our brothers and sisters passionately. This is what the Gospel means when it warns us that unless we die to ourselves we shall not truly live. Life in the Spirit involves a constant process of dying to sin, a change of heart from self-centeredness, which is the root of sin, to an attitude of self-surrendering love and service for others. Thus, long before the moment of death, "dying with Christ" refers to the life of discipleship. To die with Christ is to open one's heart to the power and to the demands of the Spirit, to become a person who is fully and fearlessly "for others," especially for the poor and the oppressed. To die with Christ is not to be spared suffering, fear or death, but it is to be filled with Christ's own Spirit, and therefore with the same courage that gave him the power and confidence to face the demands of his life and death honestly and willingly.

This truth is fundamental to all of the different ways in which theology has tried to explain the saving significance of Christ's death. Jesus does not die "for us" in the sense that he does something from which we are then exempted. His death certainly does not exempt us from dying or from the daily struggle to overcome sin. It does empower us to live with him and to die with him in hope. Because of his death, dying for the Christian can really be an act of faith, hope and love rather than something to be denied, repressed, or merely fought. In the end it can be chosen and embraced with Jesus as an act of loving trust and surrender to the One who raised Jesus from the dead.

The surrender of self in trusting love to the mystery of the other is the greatest challenge of life. It is at once terrifying and trans-fixing. It comes to its final concentration in dying. The Christian is invited to imagine death as the final, summing and consuming act of self-abandonment to the one Mystery who alone is worthy of such total trust and self-abandonment, God. It is abandon-ment both as the loving entrustment of what I have achieved and endured and as the entrustment of the deepest desire for the full-ness of life which has never found its real fulfillment. Our dying, like our living, is fundamentally an act of faith as self-entrustment. It can be a moment of grace.

As we come to the close of these reflections about Christian dying and death, I would like to say once again that we have not been speaking about the particular moment of biological death, but about a radical aspect of our living. In reflecting on death we have really been speaking about life's *end*, not merely about its finish, but about its purpose and destination. As we approach the end of our lives, each of us hears the call to surrender. It is frightful to feel one's mental and physical capacities fail; excruciat-ing to watch it happen to a loved one. It is difficult to become so dependent on others again. The surrender which death requires makes enormous demands on the whole family and community. Ministry to the dying and to those who care for the dying is so important, too important to leave to a few "professionals."

The dying, however, are not only persons who are to be cared for and supported, but also those, who by their very act of dying are prophets speaking to us. Those who feel threatened by death, who hide from it or try to deny it, *need* the dying and what they reveal to us of ourselves and of God. Their "productive" or "valuable" life is not over. They may see their dying as an inten-tional exercise of ministry and care for their loved ones and for the community. In life, especially as we are dying, we are called and empowered by the Spirit to be *martyrs*, witnesses of faithful surrender to God. Such witness does not always require words. Like Christ, Christian men and women may speak the good news in their bodies, through their wounds.

RELATED READINGS

Xavier Léon-Dufour, *Life and Death in the New Testament: The Teaching of Jesus and Paul* (San Francisco: Harper and Row, 1986) is an excellent book for biblical perspectives. Karl Rahner's thought is developed in *On the Theology of Death* (London: Burns & Oates, 1961) and presented in a more concise form in "Christian Dying" in *Theological Investigations 18* (New York: Crossroad, 1983), 226–56. Ernest Becker, *The Denial of Death* (New York: Free Press, 1973) is an extremely thought-provoking analysis from a critical Freudian perspective. Although it does not directly deal with death, William Lynch, *Images of Hope: Imagination as Healer of the Hopeless* (Notre Dame: University of Notre Dame Press, 1974) is quite relevant and full of great insight. Elizabeth Kübler-Ross, *On Death and Dying* (New York: Macmillan, 1969) has become a classic and Walter J. Smith, S.J., *Dying in the Human Life Cycle* (New York: Holt, Rinehart & Winston, 1986) offers insights from a psychologist's perspective.

9

Resurrection of the Body

In the last chapter we already began to speak about resurrection. The resurrection of the crucified Jesus is the heart of the Gospel message and the foundation of Christian faith. Nevertheless, I suspect that the word resurrection makes most Christians today think of an event in the life of Jesus which they remember at Easter rather than as something to which they themselves look forward. They would probably explain Christianity's view of an "after-life" by speaking of an immortal soul that survives death and goes to heaven or hell. This has been the common teaching of the church since earliest times. It no doubt developed as a way of responding to a serious pastoral problem concerning the fate of the faithful departed. What are Christians, who profess the resurrection of Christ, to make of the graves of their beloved dead, who do not appear to have been raised like Christ? The problem became all the more acute as belief in the Lord's imminent coming (*parousia*) faded.

The NT itself, the early cult of the martyrs and the liturgical importance of the communion of saints show that from earliest times Christians believed that the faithful dead are somehow with God. It is in this context that we can appreciate the early origin and pastoral importance of a Christian doctrine concerning the immortality of the "soul." It offered Christians a way of side-stepping the problem of resurrection (and the "delayed" *parousia*) by speaking of the present state of the departed believer's soul with God.

This doctrine is articulated and developed at Toledo (675), Lateran IV (1215), Lyons II (1274), and Vienna (1312). Benedict XII (1336) and Florence (1439) taught that the souls of the faithful, separated from the body in death, are with Christ in heaven immediately after death (or after purification in purgatory) and enjoy the beatific vision. The Second Vatican Council (LG 48-51; GS 18, 39) reaffirms the tradition, emphasizing the eschatological nature of the pilgrim church on earth and its union with the saints in heaven. The *Letter of the Sacred Congregation for the Doctrine of the Faith on Certain Questions Concerning Eschatology* (1979), appealing more to the liturgical practice of the church than to philosophical or anthropological arguments, affirms that a "soul" or "spiritual element survives and subsists after death" so that the " 'human self' subsists, *though deprived for the present of the complement of its body.*"

To the extent that union with God is conceived of in these terms, there is no insurmountable problem posed either by the corruption of the body in the grave or the fact that the expected *parousia* and general resurrection have not taken place. As a matter of fact, it would seem that as serious belief in the imminent end of the world disappeared, belief in the resurrection of the body lost all practical import. Christians began to focus instead on the salvation of their "souls," which unlike the mortal body, could "go to heaven."

There are, however, serious problems with the anthropology which underlies such teaching. It seems hard to reconcile with the church's own traditional teaching concerning the irreducible *unity* of the human person, as we have seen in an earlier chapter. Moreover, the Scriptures speak quite definitely about *resurrection* of the dead; the ancient creeds of the resurrection of the *body*. What does this mean? How is it related to the notion of the immortality of the soul? Why is a renewed appreciation of the resurrection of the body important for us today?

Biblical Background

For Israel, God is a "God of the living" not of the dead. Being in relationship with God is restricted to "this life." After death, there is at most the shadowy non-life of Sheol. After the time of the great prophets, we begin to find OT roots of belief in resurrection in the conviction that there would be a final reckoning on the "day of the Lord." Resurrection to judgment, reward or retribution, seemed to be a natural consequence not only of final moral responsibility of the individual before God, but also of God's Covenant responsibility to vindicate the faithful just who suffer so much in life at the hands of the wicked (Wisdom 3; Job 19:25-27; Dan 12:2; 2 Mac 7:9, 14). Within the Pharisaic tradition, the general resurrection was eventually seen as the ground of hope not only for Israel's vindication, but for the apocalyptic revelation of God's mercy upon all the nations.

In NT times, the resurrection of the dead was hotly disputed. On one occasion, Paul was able to get out of a difficult spot before the Sanhedrin by starting a theological free-for-all on the subject (Acts 23:6-10)! Jesus himself was confronted by the Sadducees who denied it (Mk 12:18-27). In his reply, however, it is clear that resurrection is connected not merely with the idea of just retribution, but with God's faithful love. Apart from this, Jesus does not seem to have spoken much about the resurrection directly. Neither the preceding tradition, nor Jesus' own references to resurrection can provide a real basis for our reflections. For that we must look to the resurrection of Jesus itself. Because it is something radically new, not merely an instance of a well-defined concept or belief, it alone can serve as a correct focal point.

The Resurrection of Jesus Christ

As the earliest kerygmatic formulae of the NT show, the Gospel began as the simple proclamation of an event. God has raised this man Jesus whom we have crucified (Acts 2:23f). The resurrection of Jesus is utterly unlike the assumption of Elijah into heaven or the revivification of Lazarus, who died again. The foundation of Christian faith is the testimony of those to whom the Lord showed himself, those by whom the Lord "was seen" to be alive, and alive in a new way. The Christian understanding of resurrection is really nothing more than a theological reflection upon the event and significance of Jesus' resurrection and our participation in it.

The resurrection narratives of the NT make it utterly implausible to reduce the meaning of Jesus' resurrection to an inner conviction of the disciples that Jesus' cause must and will go on. With his death, his cause and their hopes had been shattered. Something happened after Jesus "died and was buried." They found his tomb empty. Jesus himself was seen to be alive. This is the good news which enables the disciples to understand for the first time what Jesus' cause really was (Lk 24:13-35)!

Something had happened which was unlike any other event in history. In fact, it signalled the "end" of history and the beginning of a new age. The Gospel narratives present Jesus' death and resurrection, not as a personal privilege of Jesus, but as the culmination of God's action "for us and for our salvation." It is God's final act of merciful judgment on sin and death and the victorious establishment of God's reign, which Jesus had announced, enacted and identified himself with. The resurrection of Jesus is not merely a kind of extrinsic miracle which attests to his truthfulness, but God's sign that his life-unto-death for others is what divine life is all about. It is the revelation that God's divine life is the end and fulfillment (*eschaton*) of all history.

While the chief point of the appearance stories is simply the testimony to this event ("I have seen the Lord!" or "The Lord is risen indeed!"), the details of the stories are instructive as well. They make it clear that it is truly Jesus, and Jesus truly alive, who shows himself. It is not a ghost, nor merely an inner experience of the disciples, but someone with flesh and blood and an appetite (Lk 24:37-43)! His flesh still bears the marks of the nails and spear (Jn 20:27). And yet this is no ordinary flesh and blood. Jesus passes through locked doors (Jn 20:19) and vanishes suddenly (Lk 24:31). There is something different about Jesus. His closest friends, like Mary Magdalene (John 20:14f) and the disciples (Jn 21:4, 12; Lk 24:16), do not recognize him at first.

It is the *same* Jesus, who died and was buried, who is now alive. But it is clear that Jesus is not the *same*! He is not a corpse resuscitated, living as he once did. Jesus does not "return" to life in the sense of going "back" to his former way of living. Rather, through the power of the Spirit, God brings him "forward," through death, to a new fullness and intensity of life. It is really Jesus, but it is a Jesus transformed, a Jesus who, though bone of our bones and flesh of our flesh, can no longer "be held" by this world. But the empty tomb stands as a sign that this future fullness is not attained by shedding the body as worthless refuse. By virtue of God's power, the whole of Jesus' human life is saved and transformed. The proclamation concerning the resurrection of the Lord witnesses to the basic experience of faith: the Lord is alive and truly present.

Pauline Theology

The most extended reflection on resurrection in the NT is found in 1 Corinthians 15. Paul responds to those in Corinth who dismiss the idea of the resurrection of believers as ridiculous (v. 12). Presumably they prefer some sort of philosophical teaching about the immortality of the soul or believe that the gift of the Spirit in baptism gives a person a new spiritual self which is immortal. Paul argues that to deny the resurrection of the dead is to deny the resurrection of Christ himself, something which even his opponents would not be prepared to do. Christ's resurrection is proof that God has begun the divine act of saving judgment expected on the last day. He is the first fruits, then those who belong to him on the day of his *parousia* (vv. 12-20). Then the end shall appear and death, the final enemy shall be destroyed, so that God will be everything to all (vv. 22-28). He then addresses one last objection. "What kind of body will they have?" One senses the rhetorical ridicule of Paul's opponents, who believe, of course, that the dead have no body at all! For Paul, it is obvious that since personal life is bodily, the body is somehow involved in resurrection (1 Cor 6:13). It is another thing altogether to attempt to describe just what the bodiliness of the resurrection is. It cannot be merely the "flesh and blood" (v. 50) bodiliness of sinful, mortal life (*sōma psychikon*, "soulish body"). This must be transformed by God into a new mode of embodiment in the Kingdom of God (*sōma pneumatikon*, "spiritual body") in which it is no longer threatened by corruption and death (v. 44). To speak paradoxically of a "spiritual body" may not help those who are curious about details, but it does make it clear that Paul is not interested in the typically Greek contrast or division between body and soul, but between human life now (soul bodiliness) and human life as transformed in the resurrection (spirit bodiliness). He simply does not view the human person in terms of a body/soul dichotomy in which the soul is essential, the body provisional. For Paul, it is clear that since God is able to give us the body appropriate to our present existence, God will certainly give us a glorified body in the life of the resurrection.

What is so important about bodily resurrection that Paul would speak in such a paradoxical way? As the catholic biblical scholar Pheme Perkins has shown, the resurrection is not merely a future destiny of the believer but a reality that shapes Christian life even now.[1] Indeed, the resurrection of Jesus can be a source of hope and an effective pledge of *future* glory only if Christians can somehow experience the presence and activity of the risen Lord here and *now* in the power of his *Spirit* (Rom 8:9-11). Thus, it would be a mistake to think that the primary experience of the community is one of the Lord's absence. Jesus' death and exaltation do not mean that he is now utterly removed and cut off from the community. On the contrary, even as the community awaits the "return" of the one who has been "taken up," Jesus is nonetheless present and may be experienced as such in the *body* of the community as it is enlivened and formed by his Spirit. Perhaps the *parousia* of the Lord should be viewed less as the return of one who has been gone at a specific point in time (the end-point) and more as the *process* in which the presence of the Lord in the Spirit reaches final and universal fullness.

Speaking of the *body* is one way in which Paul can concretize and focus the reality and import of resurrection for the present life of the community. The body is not merely a perishable entity of no ultimate value. Because of the resurrection, the body is "for the Lord, and the Lord for the body." It is realm in which God acts, in which the Lord reigns and in which God is to be glorified (1 Cor 6:12-20). Bodily resurrection in the future means that we must take life "in the Spirit" now seriously as *bodily*. Already in Paul's time, gnosticism was a real force in some Jewish circles. By the second century it was Christianity's greatest "look-alike"

[1]Pheme Perkins, *Resurrection: New Testament Witness and Contemporary Reflection* (Garden City, NY: Doubleday and Co., 1984), especially chapter eight ("Resurrection as Jesus' Presence") and chapter nine ("Resurrection and the Future of the Christian").

opponent in a great variety of forms. If the body is forgotten in the "after-life," the "spiritual" person is likely to forget it in this life. One may not use the Spirit as an excuse for neglecting the "bodily" needs of the community or for fleeing from responsibility for the world.

Death and resurrection is *the* pattern or form of Christian life under the Lordship of Christ. In Philippians 3, Paul understands his own sufferings in this context and exhorts the community to imitate him in this regard, so that they may, even now, know Christ and "the power of his resurrection" and finally "attain the resurrection of the dead" (3:10f). Baptism seems to have been the most significant sacramental expression of this conviction and reality. The fact that Christians are enabled to "walk in newness of life" is the direct result of Christ's resurrection (Rom 6:1-11).

Finally, this pattern informs not only the lives of individual believers and the "body" of the community as a whole but the whole creation as it waits its final transformation (Romans 8). It is the power of the risen Lord, now present as the Spirit, which enables believers to live with courage and confidence in the present age.

Conclusions

Resurrection is the central metaphor used in the NT to describe the eschatological act of God in rescuing Jesus from death and glorifying him as Lord. The resurrection life is a reality which believers already begin to share with Christ in the life of the Spirit, who is God's pledge of future glory in its fullness when all creation will be made new. Bodily resurrection refers to the person and destiny of Jesus and to the life and future of believers in the *totality* of their existence. It is a way of stressing both the personal identity of the crucified and risen Lord Jesus and the continuity between the community's present life of grace and future life of glory.

It does not mean that my body will be revived (in what age or state?!) but that I, in the whole of my existence, will reach definitive and lasting fullness. It is the identity and continuity of life which is at issue, not a particular set of atoms. Even in "this life," the body I call my own is a constantly changing collection of matter. Who can say that when I die there is even a single atom which has been present from my birth? From this point of view, although the biblical idea of resurrection is *not* a doctrine about an immortal soul, it would seem to imply one, at least insofar as the church understands the soul to be the principle of personal identity and continuity in human life. Nonetheless, biblical anthropology (and modern science) demand that we view the human person holistically. The fact that human life is real only in the inseparable, irreducible totality of spiritual and corporeal dimensions means that we may not think of our final destiny in terms of souls who have no connection whatsoever to material reality.

It seems to me that we cannot really go beyond Paul, who rejected both spiritualistic and naturalistic reductions. With him we must hold that resurrection life is a healing, perfecting transformation of the whole person by God, not merely the survival of our "best self." It must be bodily in some sense, even though it is impossible to imagine how that might be. But with Paul, we must realize that the point does not lie in such idle curiosity anyway. The reason why we, with Paul, ought to speak of salvation as the *resurrection* of the dead, or with the early creeds, of the resurrection of the *body*, is because it focuses the Gospel of the cross and resurrection on the real life of persons in community, not upon souls separated from the body.

Seen in the light of a biblically based anthropology and cosmology, the body is the "real symbol" both of our interpersonal relatedness in the whole human family and of our relationship with the earth and cosmos as a whole. Thus the doctrine about the resurrection of the body is a statement about the perfection of individual human beings in the context of interpersonal and cosmic solidarity. There is no salvation apart from the body and from the world, but only as the resurrection of the body and the consummation of the world. Resurrection is the transforming perfection of bodily life, not escape from materiality. It is not real except within the whole "body" of Christ, which is a new humanity. It is not full until the whole "body" of the world is set free from bondage and God is all in all. Only then does life as "being-with-others" reach its fullness. Resurrection, therefore, is a metaphor for God's eschatological and universal saving act.

The resurrection of the body already begins now in the living, bodily action of individual men and women forgiven and empowered by grace. It is brought to some kind of definitive and victorious shape in death, which may be understood as the Lord's final coming (*parousia*) to each of us as an individual. And it looks to the final transformation of the entire world, when the Kingdom shall appear as history's end and fulfillment.

Thus, we are reminded that however important it is to understand human life and its final destiny as something which is truly personal and personally saved by God, "my" resurrection is not complete and full until the entire created world enters into its promised fullness. I will not be raised in utter fullness until the world is raised into the fullness of the Kingdom. If I die with Christ and so enter into the fullness of God's love, must not I, with God, also long for the day when all others will find their fullness in God, when God will be all in all? Entering into eternal life, while perfecting and fulfilling the individual, also fills and makes absolutely intense his or her desire for the salvation of all. Perhaps here we begin to catch a glimmer of the mystery of the communion of saints.

RELATED READING

Pheme Perkins, *Resurrection: New Testament Witness and Contemporary Reflection* (Garden City, NY: Doubleday and Co., 1984) is a brilliant and comprehensive work with an excellent bibliography. Also very helpful are Raymond Brown, *The Virginal Conception and Bodily Resurrection of Jesus* (New York: Paulist Press, 1973) and Jerome Neyrey, *The Resurrection Stories* (Wilmington, DL: Michael Glazier, 1988). A concise presentation of Karl Rahner's thought is found in the chapter entitled "The Theology of the Death and Resurrection of Jesus" in *Foundations of Christian Faith* (New York: Crossroad, 1978). Hans Urs von Balthasar, *Life out of Death* (Philadelphia: Fortress Press, 1985) is a very fine set of meditations.

10

Our Final Destiny

Traditional theology speaks of the "four last things," referring to death, judgment, heaven and hell. In the previous chapters, we have begun to touch upon them. I have already spoken about death and resurrection at some length. In this chapter I would like to consider how Christian faith understands judgment, heaven and hell as the final destiny of human beings.

Human Responsibility before God

A correct understanding of judgment is rooted in the freedom of human creatures and their responsibility before the creator. According to Genesis, human beings created in the image of God are not simply free; they are stewards of creation, and as God's partners and representatives therein, they are ultimately accountable to God. Exodus portrays the deliverance of the Hebrew slaves from Egypt and their creation as a people as God's foundational judgment, the revelation of God's loving-kindness and fidelity. First and foremost, therefore, judgment is God's saving, life-giving action on behalf of Israel, and through Israel, on behalf of all the nations. The Covenant is the central expression of God's justice and judgment. Freedom and responsibility are seen specifically in terms of Covenant fidelity and Israel perceives the consequences of its actions in the here and now events of its history. God's judgment does not pertain only to a certain moment of final reckoning on the last day. Still, it does look to a future promised by God. God's judgment, the revelation of mercy and life for God's people, promises final victory for the oppressed and defeat to all oppressors and forces of oppression. The final act of judgment on the "day of the Lord" would mean the fulfillment of the Promise and the establishment of God's Kingdom.

Christ: God's Judgment and Judge

If we turn to the NT, we find John the Baptist preaching the imminent judgment of God. Against this background, Jesus appears proclaiming the coming of God's Kingdom. Jesus preached about the judgment of God in terms familiar to his listeners. Similar to the language of the "two ways" which we find throughout the OT, we meet a whole host of images and parables which speak of the Kingdom and a final judgment with two possible outcomes. The parables of the weeds of the field, the net thrown into the sea (Matthew 13) and the judgment scene of Matthew 25 are representative examples. Acceptance of the Kingdom leads to "Abraham's bosom," a "wedding feast" or "shining like the sun." Rejection of the Kingdom leads to "outer darkness" or a "furnace of fire" where there will be "weeping and gnashing of teeth." Such texts are not literal descriptions of the future outcome, from which we might conclude that a certain number will in fact be saved, a certain number damned. Rather, they reveal that the present situation of the listeners is a time of decision. In proclaiming the faithful and final love of God for all men and women, the Gospel demands a decision which will have final, definitive results. Those who have eyes to see and ears to hear ought to choose the Lord and the life he reveals.

That Jesus preached about a final judgment is not new, but unlike the other prophets who merely pointed to the coming Kingdom as the appearance of God's judgment, he identifies himself with it. "For whoever is ashamed of me and of my words in this adulterous and sinful generation, of him or her will the Son of man also be ashamed, when he comes in the glory of his Father with the holy angels" (Mk 8:38). These words almost certainly go back to Jesus himself and indicate that final judgment is already a question of one's response to him and his words. Other versions of this text present Jesus identifying himself explicitly with this Son of Man, even if it is unlikely that Jesus himself made such a claim. They show us rather what the community believed. Jesus, the preacher of the Kingdom, *is* himself the appearance of the Kingdom, the revelation of God's judgment. Christ, therefore, is the final judge; he will speak and rule with the sovereignty of God. For the early Christians, this was a source of great confidence and joy. The coming of the Lord who would judge the living and the dead was eagerly anticipated as a day of recompense and salvation. Later piety, drawing on images from the courtroom, began to stress individual and judicial aspects. The day of judgment would be a day of fear and trembling.

Particular Judgment, General Judgment

Church teaching since the thirteenth century has focused more on the judgment of the individual person at the moment of death. Theology has referred to this as the particular judgment as distinguished from the final or general judgment at the end of the world. As far as the personal responsibility and final destiny of the individual is concerned, there is no reason to stress a distinction. Nonetheless, as we saw above, the final judgment, at least in the view of the scriptures, is something which concerns much more than a determination of the merit and guilt of individuals. More radically, it is an eschatological, transforming act of God which brings individual persons and all of history to its consummation. God fulfills the Promise and brings God's whole creation to its final fulfillment. Thus one can make a distinction between the particular judgment of individuals in death and the general judgment which constitutes the end and consummation of history.

Life under Judgment

The doctrine that human beings enter into their final destiny immediately upon death, however, does not mean that God's act of judgment is merely something that happens at the end of one's life or at the end of the world. As we have already seen, Christian faith understands death as the process in which human life attains final and definitive form. Then, in the unclouded light of God's love, we shall see our lives with complete clarity. Stripped of all masks and excuses, each will have to judge what he or she has really become in life. Each will encounter God as one who, in the free decisions and actions of his or her life, has made a "fundamental option" for or against God and, therefore, for or against his or her very self as a creature destined to find life in God. The judgment of God, therefore, is not a sentence imposed from without. We may think of it as the act in which God ratifies the judgment we ourselves have made in the concrete choices of our lives.

In this sense, judgment is already taking place in our response to Jesus. As the Fourth Gospel reminds us, even now we are judged by the Son, his Word and our response to it (Jn 3:18ff). Even more pointedly, Matthew tells us that we stand before the judge in the presence of the neighbor, especially the least of the brothers and sisters, the poor (Mt 25:40, 45). It is interesting, however, that in the story, even the righteous did not recognize the Lord in their works of mercy. The criterion of judgment has nothing to do with religious ritual, observance or "experiences." How clearly and radically Jesus refocused the significance of the Law and judgment! What counts is clothing the naked, visiting the sick, feeding the hungry, what were once called the corporal and spiritual works of mercy. That is where judgment is taking place.

Judgment: The Revelation of God's Mercy

Judgment, therefore, implies responsibility before God for ourselves and for our fellow human beings. Paul warned believers that they must work out their salvation with fear and trembling (Phil 2:12). And yet he encouraged them to rely completely on the faithful love of God shown to us in Christ who died for us while we were yet sinners (Rom 5:8). Christ himself *is* God's judgment. Thus, God's "final" judgment about us is not something which is still completely unknown or uncertain. If anything, it is *our* final judgment about God which remains ambiguous! The whole point of revelation is that in Jesus, the unchangeable truth of God's unbreakable love for each and every one of us is finally and completely visible. This is the one and only absolutely infallible truth of Christian faith. The ever-greater measure, power and scope of God's grace in Christ (Romans 5) convinces Paul that God is and has always been for us and against everything that could possibly separate us from God (Romans 8). In this sense we know precisely where we stand in God's eyes.

Destined to be Saved

Indeed, throughout the NT, alongside the images and parables of judgment which dramatically heighten the sense of urgency and underline the possibility of being lost or condemned, we find many texts which express the trust and hope that we may have in the universal saving will of God. It is the "mystery of God's will" to unite all things in Christ (Eph 1:9f; Col 1:20). God does not wish anyone to perish (2 Pet 3:9). When Jesus is lifted up, he will draw all women and men to himself (Jn 12:32). It is the Father's will that not one should be lost (Jn 6:39).

It is true that according to church teaching, one cannot know with certainty whether one will be saved (that would be presumption) or damned (that would be despair). But this does not deny God's gracious, sovereign and universal saving will. Nor should it call into question the *hope* which we ought to have for the salvation of all women and men. Indeed, faith in the God who wills the salvation of all seems to *demand* that we really and realistically hope for the salvation of all. As Balthasar and Rahner remind us, what Christian faith cannot *know* with certainty, it can *hope for* with assurance.

But God's judgment, an act of eternally faithful love which does not and could not abandon us in our sin or death, is not merely a unilateral declaration unrelated to our free response. God's love for us, as revealed in the judgment of Christ, is the prior foundation of our very existence. It is not the result of, nor is it merited by, our actions. It does not depend on us. If anything we depend on it. But love cannot force. Love can only offer. It can only surrender itself to the beloved. God's judgment is a gracious offer of life in its fullness and at the same time a plea made by God in the human flesh and blood of Christ to accept it. As such it demands our response, and everything hangs upon it. It is an offer, we might say, which made definitively "once and for all," must be embraced by us all in our ordinary lives. Thus the response of faith means both confidence in the power of God's love and courage to allow God's kind of justice to inform my everyday life.

From the very beginning, church teaching has underscored the essential role of human freedom in responding to God's action in Christ. This was the valid concern of Pelagius in the early controversy about the relationship between God's grace and human freedom. Unfortunately the teaching of his orthodox opponent, Augustine, on double predestination had an enormous impact through the Middle Ages and down to the Reformers and Jansenists. Strictly speaking, since God has created us for only one reason, to share God's own divine life, we must say that God has predestined us for that life and for that life alone. Therefore, heaven and hell are not two equally possible, alternative "destinations."

The confidence for the day of judgment of which we have spoken is the fruit of love which casts out fear. Like all true love, it is not something which comes to rest in itself. It shows its authenticity in its power to enable men and women to turn from sin in order to love one another fearlessly after the example of Christ. And when we are conscious of the many times we have failed or refused to love, faith in God's love gives us the courage one day finally to entrust our imperfect lives to be judged by the One who is not Yes and No, but always Yes (2 Cor 1:19).

Heaven and Hell

As far as the final destiny of human beings is concerned, there are really only two possibilities: the acceptance of God's gracious gift of divine life or the rejection of it. In the language of traditional Christian piety, one goes either to heaven or to hell. What does this really mean?

Scriptural language and much teaching and preaching based on it seem to speak of places of eternal reward ("heaven," "Kingdom of God") and punishment ("gehenna"). Heaven is described as a wedding feast; hell as a place of fire, darkness and torment. Such language must not be taken literally. Heaven is not simply an earthly paradise regained, a sort of garden of earthly delights. Hell is not a raging inferno with flames of varying temperature and tortures for various sins. Heaven and hell are not really "places" at all but theological ways of talking about our personal relationship with God as it reaches its final end and destiny. God, as Augustine said, is our final "place." Balthasar proposes that God offering God's self in love is judgment; God accepted and loved is heaven; God rejected and lost is hell. Jesus Christ is the revelation that God, and not some other thing (as "reward" or "punishment") is our final end.[1] Jesus Christ, truly divine, truly human, is God's final self-communication to the world as its own deepest fulfillment. Heaven and hell, therefore, are essentially Christological concepts which describe the life of the risen, glorified Jesus and the world's participation in or rejection of it.

Thus, the life of heaven, the life of the Kingdom has already begun in the grace of Christ which constitutes the believing community. The life of grace "on earth" and life "in heaven" are different in degree, not in kind. In one sense, heaven is *God*; heaven is the self-communication of God's own life to the human world through Jesus Christ. In another sense, we may say that heaven is the *world* brought to its final glory in and by God's saving love. This is the heart of Jesus' proclamation concerning the Kingdom. The Kingdom of God, or as Matthew often puts it, the Kingdom of Heaven, does not refer to a different, (otherworldly?) place where God rules. Such a thought would be foreign to the basic OT understanding of God's Lordship. Israel confesses God to be the Lord of creation and more particularly, the Lord of its own history and future as a people. Jesus' proclamation is firmly rooted in this tradition. He does not tell people what they must do in order to "go to heaven." He announces (and is) God's coming and exhorts the people to open up their hearts and lives to God's reign.

Jesus spoke of the Kingdom as present among us and Christian believers may see the contours of this Kingdom wherever men and women allow the sacrificial love and justice so evident in Christ's life to shape their own lives. Since the Kingdom has not appeared in its fullness, it is an already/not yet paradox. Since it refers to the *final* end and perfection of the world, it would be wrong to identify completely any particular place or time, any

[1]Hans Urs von Balthasar, "Some Points of Eschatology," *Word and Redemption* (New York: Herder and Herder, 1965) 154.

particular social, political or religious structure with the Kingdom as "heaven on earth." The final fullness to which the world as a whole is called cannot appear in the normal course of history, while the world is yet on the way. Only when God, in a final transforming act, takes the world to God's self, will we be able to see "earth as heaven." Just as the world has its absolute origin from God and "from nothing" else, so too, it is finally dependent upon God for its fulfillment and final meaning. This is the basic significance of God's Lordship in Scripture. Only God, not we humans, can bring the world to its perfection. To be sure, God does not accomplish this alone, but in and through us. The paradigm for Christian faith remains the life, death and resurrection of Jesus.

It is remarkable that while the NT is full of images and parables about the Kingdom of heaven, we find very few descriptions of hell. Jesus preached the coming of God's Kingdom, not the existence of hell. Often Christian preaching seems to have gotten things just the other way around. Perhaps this is because the reality of evil is so obvious. Perhaps the power of sin and death make it nearly impossible to imagine, let alone believe in, the sort of Kingdom which Jesus preaches.

While Jesus did not teach the factual existence of hell, his words and parables remind us pointedly that hell is a deadly *possibility* for the unrepentant sinner. Sin is always a real possibility for free creatures. We already saw that sin means "missing the mark," turning away from God and the life with God for which we were made. Hell may be viewed as a final fixation in sin. It is the self-centeredness, hatred, pride and greed of sin, grown and hardened into radical self-isolation and rejection of God. If heaven may be thought of as God's creating, sustaining and transforming action brought to its fullness, then hell may be viewed as a kind of "anti-creation" on the part of the creature who completely refuses God's life and love.

As such, hell is not a place of punishment prepared *by God* for those who disobey. It is constructed by the creature, or better, it is the self-destruction of the creature who chooses to remain in sin. We are not cast into flames prepared by another and existing before us. There is no physical outer darkness, flame or worm. As Origen suggested, each sinner ignites the "fire" of his or her own hell. Hell is "in" such a person; people are not "in" hell.

Unlike the Kingdom of heaven, a reality which already exists, and to which we are called, hell does not exist "before" or "apart" from each and every individual sinner. In fact, it is really a way of describing the utter isolation of the one who attempts finally and radically to cut him or herself off from all love. The condemned would not be in hell "together"; each would be a hell unto himself or herself.

Even as a possibility, hell, as freely chosen self-destructive isolation, remains radically absurd. Moreover, since God's love for us is absolute and unconditional, rather than a reward for the good we do, it can never weaken or be withheld as a result of our sin. Sin, even "mortal" sin, does not make God love us less or desire our reconciliation less.

This has led some theologians to suggest that hell, as the rejection of God's love, can really have only a sort of "one-sided" existence, on the side of the one engaged in the absurd attempt to sustain the hell he or she has created. Balthasar has challenged the typical understanding of hell in light of the mystery of Holy Saturday.[2] He suggests that the true meaning of the "descent into hell" is not the triumphant entrance of the victorious Christ liberating the just, who have been trapped there awaiting the appearance of the promised Messiah. Holy Saturday, he suggests, is the mystery of Jesus' descent into the death of sin, his complete and loving identification with sinners who have abandoned God. This means in a certain sense that in Jesus, God surrenders himself into what might be called hell, in order to show us that there is absolutely nothing which can destroy God's love for us and God's presence with and for us. In Christ, God is with all sinners "in hell," so that whatever hell is, it is something which involves the sinner's rejection of God, and not God's rejection of the sinner. Whatever the power of human freedom is to reject God, it is not strong enough to prevent God from being truly present in unbreakable love to the sinner. And according to Balthasar, we may hope

[2]Medard Kehl and Werner Löser, (eds.), *The Von Balthasar Reader* (New York: Crossroad, 1982), 150–53, 420–22. See also the new English translation of Balthasar's *Mysterium Paschale* (Edinburgh: T & T Clark, 1990).

that the power of misguided freedom is not strong enough to resist the compassionate presence of the powerless crucified Christ.

In light of all of this, we may say that heaven and hell are not merely two equally possible alternatives. Does not the NT give us every reason in view of the victorious power of God's love, to view the very possibility of hell as the most radical anomaly? This was the question which so plagued Origen and others like him who, though following good instincts, were inclined to the exaggeration of asserting the final salvation of all. Is this such an exaggeration, though? To be a believer means to believe in the final victory of God's love in Jesus Christ over sin and death, and *then* to acknowledge, in the life of faith, hope and love, the radical responsibility that our free response entails and our ultimate accountability for it before God. Not the other way around! Christianity is not primarily a moral order which preaches final accountability. That is nothing new. It is the announcement of the good news of God's saving judgment in Christ. It seems perfectly consonant with *faith* in the power of God's love to *doubt* that human sin (or the freedom which makes it possible) could finally be stronger. Faith in the victory of God's saving love is the foundation of our hope that all will be saved.

RELATED READING

Michael Schmaus, *Dogma 6: Justification and the Last Things* (Kansas City: Sheed and Ward, 1977) and Joseph Ratzinger, *Eschatology, Death and Eternal Life* (Washington: Catholic University of America Press, 1988) offer comprehensive treatment of church teaching. Hans Urs von Balthasar, *Dare We Hope "That All Men be Saved"?* (San Francisco: Ignatius Press, 1988) is a superb and enlightening treatment of Christian hope. Other themes of eschatology are treated in "Some Points of Eschatology" in *Explorations in Theology 1: The Word Made Flesh* (San Francisco: Ignatius Press, 1989), 255–77 [reprint of *Word and Redemption* (New York: Herder and Herder, 1965), 147–75] and in Medard Kehl, S.J. and Werner Löser, S.J. (eds.), *The Von Balthasar Reader* (New York: Crossroad, 1982). On final con-

summation see Karl Rahner, "The Theological Problems Entailed
in the Idea of the 'New Earth' " and "Immanent and Transcendent Consummation of the World" in *Theological Investigations
10* (New York: Herder and Herder, 1973), 260-72, 273-89.

11

Christian Living

Having considered the different key dimensions of human existence as seen by Christian faith, I would like, in this final chapter, to focus on a few issues basic to Christian *spirituality*: (1) Christian life as discipleship, (2) vocation and the "will of God" for the individual and (3) discernment and the Christian imagination.

Discipleship

At the end of the Gospel of Matthew, Jesus commands the eleven disciples to go and "make disciples of all nations, baptizing them in the name of the Father and of the Son and of the Holy Spirit, teaching them to observe all that I have commanded you" (28:19f). I suspect, however, that most catholics, when hearing the word disciple, think of persons described in the NT rather than themselves. To be sure, they have been baptized and instructed as to the importance of moral, ritual and doctrinal observance. There are certain "Dos" and "Don'ts." The former will be rewarded, the latter punished. Too often, this has resulted in a spirituality which is other-worldly and preoccupied with an individualistic morality of private virtue and "obeying the rules."

But the Gospel is not primarily a revelation of moral rules, liturgical rubrics or divine truths. It is the revelation that God's justice is self-surrendering, forgiving love, embodied in the Kingdom which God has established in Jesus Christ. The Gospel calls us to become his disciples, to share in his mission of transforming the world according to the norm of God's justice. We should think of Christian life in terms of *discipleship*, not observance. We have been reconciled to God in Christ and given the "ministry of reconciliation" (2 Cor 5:18). Grace and mission, holiness and service are inseparable, two aspects of the one Spirit. Perhaps Paul, more than any other NT writer, saw that God's grace (*charis*) is never private. It is a gift (*charisma*) given for the common good. The Spirit of God's love leads to freedom and becomes visible in loving service, not in religious observance (Gal 5:13). In the Gospels we see that it is the Spirit who fills Jesus, makes him holy and leads him in his mission. The same Spirit, promised by Jesus, poured out upon the disciples, constitutes the church in its holiness and empowers it in its mission. We have not been called to follow rules, as necessary as they may be, but to follow a person, Jesus Christ. To follow Christ as a disciple does not mean that we merely imitate him, but that we *participate* in his very life and mission. Christian discipleship means mission and ministry.

Life in the Spirit, therefore, is not primarily a question of private virtue and observance but of love, active in service. Christian discipleship will always manifest both a mystical and a prophetic dimension. We are called to love God whole-heartedly and our neighbor as ourselves (Mt 22:37-40). This is clear in the lives of the saints. Genuine efforts to be one with the Lord necessarily lead to a deeper involvement in the Lord's mission in and for the world. Above all, we must care for the least of our brothers and sisters; they are the ones with whom the Lord most closely identifies himself.

I believe that it is more important than ever to recover an understanding of Christian living as *mission* and *ministry*. Only if we realize that this is the heart of Christian existence, will we be able to see the other dimensions of the life of faith in their proper perspective. The church, in the Word it preaches, the Sacraments it celebrates, the teaching it gives and the moral guidance it offers, exists only as a way of incarnating the Spirit of Jesus' life and mission in the lives of believers. None of these are ends in themselves.

This may sound strange to many catholics. I would venture to guess that most would not spontaneously think of themselves as ministers or as persons having a mission. Vatican II, with its renewed emphasis upon the role of the laity ("Decree on the Apostolate of the Laity"), stressed that all believers share in the one Christian vocation, the call to discipleship. The church is not supposed to be a place where only a representative few take the Gospel seriously or where a small group of professional disciples (the clergy) provide religious services for the much larger mass of non-professionals (the laity). By virtue of one Lord, one faith and one baptism, the whole church is a priestly people called upon to witness and minister to the Gospel of the Kingdom.

This welcome development has led to the growth and growing importance of "lay ministry," which will continue to enrich the church through a variety of new forms. It has contributed to a profound renewal of spiritual life. Vocation is no longer understood narrowly to refer to a divine call to the priesthood or "religious life." Vast numbers of lay men and women are making Ignatian retreats and receiving spiritual direction. They seek to discern the presence and call of the Spirit in the specifics of their lives. Christian life is understood as on-going call to discipleship in all its concrete dimensions. As a result, the notion of vocation, together with the issue of God's will and discernment of that will touch the heart of practical Christian living.

Vocation and the Will of God

The experience and language of vocation are deeply rooted in the Bible and in the life of the church. On its most basic level, it is an expression of faith that God is present and active in our world and that we are called in some way to participate in God's saving work.

But in what sense does God call? How can one talk meaningfully about God's will and discernment of it? According to the NT, God wills the salvation of all men and women and calls them to personal fulfillment in God's own divine life. In theology this has been called the "general" or "universal" will of God. Beyond this, is there a "specific" or "special" will of God for given individuals? Does God call each person to a specific way of life? As I face an important decision in life and pray to discern what it is that God wills me to do, must I believe that only one of the options is "what God wills"?

Certainly the Scriptures assume that God calls some individuals in specific and often rather dramatic ways. Many believers throughout history have experienced God as calling them to a particular way of life or to a particular course of action. I can see no reason to deny outright that God has called or calls certain individuals in particular ways. But the experiences of the people recounted in biblical stories, or the lives of many of the saints, seem to bear little resemblance to the ordinary lives of most Christians, who may not "hear" much from God at all, who do not have the benefit of miraculous interventions or angelic annunciations. Even assuming that I might be called by God to a certain way of life, decision or course of action, I must ask how God might make this call known. If the "Word of the Lord" came to the prophets, how does it come to me, to us today? What could it mean to say that God wills a certain way of life for me or a certain course of action in a given situation? How could I discern what it might be?

At the very least, God's will and call are *specific* in the sense that God's gift of life in fullness concerns every human being personally. God does not desire the well-being of the world as a kind of abstract generality. God desires the life of each and every creature. Thus, even before I wonder whether God has something in particular which God wants me to do, I may view my very self as that which God wills. I myself, as this particular, unique creature, in the totality of my being, with my particular talents, in the reality of my freedom, both its limitations and possibilities in this particular time and place in history, in the abiding significance of my past actions and the open-endedness of the future, and not merely some added task or action which I can accept or refuse, am God's "specific will."

We have already seen that the central hallmark of human life is *freedom*. God's will and gracious love are expressed precisely in the creation of creatures who are truly free. This is quite remarkable. God shares God's own autonomy with human beings. The fullness of life which God wills for us would have to entail the perfection of, not the frustration or destruction of, human freedom. God's specific will for each and all of us must be precisely the perfection of our freedom. God created us simply out of love and desires nothing more than the fulfillment of a freely shaped human world in that love. This suggests that in God's utterly free and freeing love, God has not determined in advance the particular decisions we ought to make or the specific shape our life paths should take, but God is "determined" that our freedom really be freed from all that prevents it from operating, and so come to its fulfillment.

Human freedom must itself be freed from sin. This, it seems to me, is the reason why the Bible often warns us that God's ways are not our ways. Our actions will be most free when they are in tune with God's fundamental desire and creative activity for the life and freedom of the world, which we believe to be revealed and victoriously established in Jesus. Since freedom itself is a capacity for loving relationship, we are most free when we are "in tune" with God's creative call to love, when we live "in the Spirit." Like good jazz players improvising together, we are invited to enter into the theme of God's saving action in ways that are genuinely unpredictable, free and novel. Christ, God's tune, is not some pre-determined exercise we are called upon to repeat exactly or imitate slavishly, but a melody which is made of freely chosen harmonies in the Spirit. If we "go with the flow" we shall experience our own free creativity as God's will; if we ignore or try to fight God's theme, we shall find empty patterns, broken rhythms and frustration, not real freedom and harmony.

May we not imagine that God's specific will for each of us is simply the unique personal life and freedom which God has blessed us with in the Spirit, full of countless, undetermined possibilities within the promised fullness of the Kingdom? God wills that all men and women take possession of and responsibility for their freedom and is delighted when we do. May we not imagine that God is truly glorified when, in the power of the Spirit, human beings have the courage and confidence to choose freely the particular contours which loving service will take in the flesh and blood of their lives?

Discernment: Inspiration and Imagination

The real issue, therefore, is not so much what God wants. We know that. God wishes the Kingdom to come in its fullness. The real issue is: *what do I want*? What do I truly desire? Do I really desire the life and freedom which God has given me? Do we really desire the life of the Kingdom which Jesus preaches and establishes? The person and preaching of Jesus touch the deepest desire for life and fullness in the human heart, and reveal that this life was always God's desire and gift for us, a gift that is only real in the act of loving. The experience of God's gracious love in the Spirit is what elicits our deepest desires. If I really desire this life then I will begin to wonder how I can most fully embrace it and give it flesh in the concrete circumstances of my life. This context includes, of course, not only my own particular talents, interests, needs and desires, but also the needs and possibilities of the world in which I live.

If we approach our lives in relationship with God in this fashion, then discernment of God's will in a given situation becomes less a question of determining and obeying a specific, pre-ordained plan and more a free act of imagination with God in the Spirit. One of the central, and most astounding, characteristics of our relationship with God is the real mutuality of grace. God, Creator and Lord, freely chooses us to be true partners and does what all true love does: communicates real freedom.[1] In Jesus, God wishes to reveal God's eternal passion and finally victorious hope for the world and to share this love and desire with us. If we are rooted in the reality of God's love and hope for the real future of the world, then God invites us to imagine what we can do to help form this future. As long as we are rooted in this love, St. Augustine reminds us, we may do as we wish (*ama et fac quod vis*). Since God is love, God wants us to imagine freely and choose to do what we want to do. The only command (and it was first a gift) is love. Jesus calls his disciples friends, not servants, and encourages them to expect the Father to give them whatever they ask in his name (Jn 15:15ff). Whatever we ask! This is an invitation that leads us to pay attention to our deepest and truest desires. It encourages us to let our desire for God and for the salvation of God's world set our imaginations free. This, it seems to me, is why, in his *Spiritual Exercises*, Ignatius puts so much stress on

---

[1]William F. Lynch, *Images of Hope: Imagination as the Healer of the Hopeless* (Notre Dame: University of Notre Dame Press, 1974) 172f.

the desires of the free and passionate heart as a way of discovering God's will. Men and women are usually more successful in discerning prayer if, with Jesus, they pay attention to their real desires and fears, than if they simply ask God to tell them what they are supposed to do.

Prayer plays a crucial role. Its purpose, in this view of things, is not to ask God to tell us what to do. It is not simply a waiting to hear God speak to us, even though there is a perfectly legitimate and necessary sense in which prayer involves God's Word and demands an attitude of waiting. I understand prayer here to mean an attentiveness of the Christian imagination to the realities and voices of the world, striving to see the Kingdom.

It cannot do this, of course, unless it has learned how to recognize the Kingdom. This is where the Scriptures play an essential role. It seems to me that the Scriptures are not meant merely to teach us certain facts about God, the world and Christian life. They are meant, rather, to inspire our imaginations, enabling us to recognize the inner heart and outer contours of the Kingdom. Hearing the Word is an act of the heart; discerning it is an act of the imagination. The stories about Jesus, his words and deeds permit the believer to develop a sensibility for the Kingdom. We contemplate Jesus, consider how he relates to God and to the men and women around him, what he says, what happens to him. This can enable us to imagine our lives in a much different way and help us to develop an ability to discern the presence of the Lord's Spirit in the ever-changing circumstances of our present lives. Thus, we use the Scriptures correctly when we allow them to change our way of looking at and thinking about the world, not when we try to find in them the correct solution to a particular problem or the divine will in a given situation.

People often come to daily prayer or periodic retreats with a particular issue which they want resolved and are unhappy or impatient when nothing seems to happen. They need to be encouraged to let go of the issue and let what happens happen. Often it is precisely a change of thinking or imagining that is needed before they can approach the particular issue fruitfully. I believe Ignatius understood this exactly and that this is why he gives such importance to contemplation (looking, wondering and savoring) over meditation (trying to figure it out, analyze the meaning or derive the moral truth). The *Spiritual Exercises* are a school not only of desire but of the imagination.

The work of the Spirit is precisely the sort of *metanoia* which involves the heart and the imagination. It is one central way in which Christian men and women may put on the mind of Christ Jesus (Phil 2:5). In this simple, but absolutely basic sense, the Scriptures are inspired because through them, Christians will discover the Spirit inspiring their imaginations. It seems to me that if Christ really does live in us, then the imagination is the special realm of the Spirit. The mystery of this sort of contemplation lies in the fact that we are changed by what we see. The *form* of Jesus and the Kingdom begins to *inform* and *transform* us. This is the work of the Spirit (2 Cor 3:18). As a result, we begin to have something like the "common sense" of faith which enables us to imagine in a Christian way. The Spirit usually inspires us in prayer, not by giving us the correct answer or God's pre-determined decision but by setting our imaginations free.

So inspired, we are able to look at the world and our lives in the world in a different way. The Scriptures, like everything in the church, are for the world, not for themselves. They are meant to train our eyes and hearts to contemplate the world as God's Kingdom and ourselves as ministers of this Kingdom. This requires a great act of imagination. Its power comes from Christ's resurrection, the revelation that God's love and life *is* victorious over death and sin. That is what sets the imagination free and empowers it for the work of the Kingdom here and now.

I know of no one who has better explored the connection between hope, imagination and freedom than William Lynch, especially in his book *Images of Hope*. Faith, as a sharing in God's own hope and love for the world, enables us to stay with the real problems and tragedies of our lives because it refuses to absolutize them. Seeing things with the "mind of God," as it were, it knows that nothing is absolute except the victory of God's saving, transforming love. It can, therefore, imagine *something* (not nothing, not everything) which it can realistically do, even if that often means waiting in hope and solidarity. But then waiting is always a great act of imagination.

In the real world of our everyday lives, and in the problems of a world which seem to overwhelm us, the process of discernment is an act of *realistic* imagination. It must be rooted in reality. It requires the same sort of information and competence which we expect in all areas of life. It takes seriously the real talents and needs, strengths and weaknesses of the persons involved. But rooted in reality, it is truly free to imagine. I do not believe that God prescribes our concrete choices. But through the inspiring Spirit, God equips us with a variety of gifts which in an infinite number of ways can contribute to the common good (1 Corinthians 12). If the Spirit makes us dead to the Law (Gal 2:19-21) and calls us to freedom (Gal 5:13), then the Spirit's inspiration cannot be the announcement of a pre-determined plan of God. This would amount to a new "law." But where the Spirit is, there is freedom (2 Cor 3:17).

What I am suggesting is that however we might understand God's will, we should seek to find it revealed in our deepest desires. If in this context, a particular object of choice, course of action, or way of life is experienced as a concrete way of accepting and responding to this radical orientation in freedom to God, then it may be called "God's will" for me or my "vocation." Here it is more important to consider whether such a specific decision can truly sustain and be sustained by the unconditioned desire for God rather than to assign too much significance to the suddenness or sheer intensity of feeling as a sign of the Spirit and God's will. The believer may say that in such an experience of desire he or she has "heard God's call" or been "led by the Spirit." However, common sense and honest piety will perhaps make us hesitant to invoke God's authority to legitimate a personal decision.

Such desires are the force and power of the Christian imagination, which as I understand it, is perhaps the central dimension of the freedom which marks our life in the Spirit. As free and absolutely open to God, we are created to desire, to imagine and to hope. In Jesus, we see that the dynamism of our desire, imagination and hope has its source in God and finds its final fulfillment in God's own divine life. We are thus uniquely able to be God's partners in the creation and salvation of the world.

RELATED READING

For a collection of shorter reflections on different aspects of Christian life see Karl Rahner, *The Practice of Faith: A Handbook of Contemporary Spirituality* (New York: Crossroad, 1983). His article "Dialogue with God?" in *Theological Investigations 18* (New York: Crossroad, 1983), 122–31, suggests that our very being is God's first "word" to us and therefore basic to any understanding of prayer. Hans Urs Von Balthasar, *Engagement with God* (London: SPCK, 1975) offers fine perspectives on discipleship. Roger Haight, *Foundational Issues in Jesuit Spirituality. Studies in the Spirituality of Jesuits 19/4* (St. Louis: The Seminar on Jesuit Spirituality, September 1987) presents a very insightful interpretation of Ignatian spirituality from the perspective of M. Blondel's philosophy of action. Of the many recent books on discernment, William A. Barry, S.J., *Paying Attention to God: Discernment in Prayer* (Notre Dame: Ave Maria Press, 1990) is one of the very best. See also his excellent use of John Macmurray's thought in "Toward a Theology of Discernment" in *The Way Supplement* 64 (Spring 1989), 129–40. On faith as imagination see William F. Lynch, S.J., *Images of Faith* (Notre Dame: University of Notre Dame Press, 1973); on desire and the imagination, *Images of Hope: Imagination as the Healer of the Hopeless* (Notre Dame: University of Notre Dame Press, 1974) by the same author.

CPSIA information can be obtained
at www.ICGtesting.com
Printed in the USA
FSHW011954190122
87793FS

9 780814 657560